SO-AXI-892

# Encyclopedia of
# CREATIVE
# COOKING

## Volume 6
## Pork, Ham & Sausages

**Editors for U.S. editions**
**Steve Sherman and Julia Older**

# ECB Enterprises Inc.

# All about Pork
*Sautéed Pork Cutlets*

Pork has a distinctive flavor which is quite different from other meats. As well as tasty roasts and chops, there are bacon, ham and many types of sausage.

### Choosing Pork

The lean meat should always be pale pink in color, without gristle and firm to the touch. It should be marbled a little with milky-white fat, and the outer fat should be firm and white. If you are buying a ham with skin or rind, make sure that there are no hairs and that it is not too thick. If you like crackling on your roast, ask the butcher to score the rind for you.

### Storing Pork

Pork is available all year round, fresh or frozen. Of course, if you have a freezer you would be well advised to buy in bulk. Roasts and chops will store in a freezer for about 4 months. Pork can be stored in a refrigerator for 2-3 days, or in a cool place for about 24 hours.

### Cuts of Pork

Pork is available in a variety of cuts and should always be cooked thoroughly. It can be roasted, grilled, broiled, fried, casseroled, cured, boiled and made into sausages. Here are the best-known cuts:

**Loin:** This is usually considered to be the choicest cut. It is also the most expensive. It can be roasted whole on the bone or boned, rolled and stuffed. It is also cut up into loin and rib chops. When roasting loin, allow ½ lb. on the bone per person, and 4-6 ozs. boned per person.

**Ham:** This is another expensive cut which is lean and tender. It is usually roasted either on the bone or boned and stuffed. It comes from the top end of the hind leg and can also be cut into steaks.

**Leg:** This is a very large roast which is often cut in two and then roasted. It can be roasted on the bone or stuffed and rolled. Generally, it has more flavor when roasted on the bone.

**Spare Ribs:** These are usually associated with Chinese and Oriental cooking. However, they are growing more popular in the West. They are usually roasted, marinated, or grilled or broiled. They should not be confused with rib chops, which come from the loin.

**Chops:** Rib and loin chops both come from the loin and are about 1 inch thick. They are usually grilled, broiled, fried or baked.

**Cutlets:** These lean pieces of meat are taken from the spare rib and have very little bone. Like chops, they can be fried, grilled, broiled or casseroled.

**Blade:** This is a cheaper cut which can be roasted or braised on or off the bone.

**Belly:** This is a very fatty cut which can be roasted entirely or cut into slices. Because it is so fat, it is cheap and sold either fresh or salted.

**Shoulder Hock:** This cut comes from the foreleg and is sold both fresh and salted. It is suitable for roasting, braising and stewing. If you are a crackling lover, this is the cut for you as it has a very large area of rind.

**Suckling Pig:** This is a young pig which is slaughtered between three weeks and two months. It can be spit-roasted.

### Sauces and Flavorings

Pork is traditionally served with applesauce. Spices such as cloves and paprika go well with pork in either a marinade or a tart apple sauce. Herbs such as thyme, sage, rosemary and garlic all enhance the flavor of pork. Pork is a favorite meat in oriental dishes and is often served with ginger, soy sauce or pineapple. You can make a delicious marinade for a roast or chops with these ingredients. Or why not try cooking your roast the Italian way? Just make some small cuts in the lean meat and insert some slivers of garlic. Sprinkle with oregano and roast as normal. The end result tastes and looks delicious. Or you can try making a sticky glaze for a pork roast with honey, orange or pineapple juice and spices such a powdered cloves, ginger or cinnamon.

# Chops and Cutlets

Both loin and rib pork chops come from the loin. Pork chops can be broiled, fried or casseroled in many different ways. In this section, we give you recipes for all three. Pork chops are most economical when served in a sauce or casserole to make them go further.

## Fruity Pork Chops

**four 6-oz. pork chops**
**salt and pepper**
**¼ cup oil**
**pinch oregano**
**½ sweet red pepper, cut in strips**
**½ cup long grain rice**
**½ lb. seedless green grapes, halved**

**1** Sprinkle the pork chops with salt and freshly ground black pepper.

**2** Heat the oil in a skillet and gently fry the chops until brown on both sides. Sprinkle in the oregano.

**3** Add the strips of red pepper and sauté until soft.

**4** Meanwhile, cook the rice in boiling salted water until tender, but still firm.

**5** Add the halved grapes to the pork and peppers and heat through.

**6** Arrange the rice on a heated serving dish and arrange the chops in the center. Spoon the peppers and grapes over the top and serve.

*Serves 4*

*Fruity Pork Chops are served on a bed of plain rice with sautéed strips of red pepper and juicy green grapes*

# Barbecued Pork Cutlets

¼ cup oil
6 pork cutlets
¼ cup butter
1 small onion, chopped
½ cup water
2 tablespoons brown sugar
½ teaspoon prepared mustard
salt and pepper
1 tablespoon vinegar
1 tablespoon tomato paste
2 tomatoes, skinned, seeded
 and chopped
1 teaspoon Worcestershire sauce
⅓ cup catsup
pinch paprika

**1** Heat the oil and fry the pork cutlets until well browned on both sides.

**2** Meanwhile, make the barbecue sauce. Melt the butter in a saucepan and sauté the onion until soft. Add the water and stir in the brown sugar, mustard, seasoning and vinegar. Bring to a boil, then simmer for 5 minutes.

**3** Add all the remaining ingredients, stir well and simmer for 15 minutes.

**4** Serve the pork cutlets with the barbecue sauce on a bed of plain boiled rice.

*Serves 6*

**Tips:** You can make the sauce more appealing by adding sliced mushrooms or peppers. If you like red-hot food, why not add a few drops of hot sauce? Or you can make a more fruity version with cooked plums, pineapple or fresh chopped peaches and apricots.

You can remove the meat from the chops, of course, and use it skewered as kebabs. Or why not try marinating the chops in soy sauce, pineapple juice, oil and garlic for a more oriental flavor?

*Pork in Cider brings the flavor of the countryside to your dinner table with its fresh vegetables and fruity taste*

# Pork in Cider

½ cup oil
2 carrots, diced
2 onions, diced
1 clove garlic, crushed
2 shallots, chopped
1 branch celery, thinly sliced
½ cup flour
3 tomatoes, skinned, seeded,
 and chopped
1¼ cups cider
bouquet garni
1 cup canned creamed corn
salt and pepper
six ½-lb. pork cutlets
1 tablespoon chopped parsley

**1** Heat half of the oil in a saucepan and gently sauté the carrots, onions, garlic, shallots and celery until tender.

**2** Sprinkle in half of the flour, stir and cook for 1 minute. Add the tomatoes and cider and bring to a boil. Add the bouquet garni and

corn and season with salt and pepper. Simmer for 15-20 minutes.

**3** Coat the cutlets in the remaining seasoned flour and heat the rest of the oil in a pan. Pan fry the cutlets for about 10 minutes until browned on both sides.

**4** Preheat the oven to 350 °F.

**5** Remove the cutlets from the pan and arrange in an ovenproof dish. Cover with the sauce and check the seasoning. Bake in the covered ovenproof dish for 20 minutes.

**6** Sprinkle with parsley and serve with boiled new potatoes.

*Serves 6*

**Tip:** If you have no cider, you can always use apple juice or white wine or a mixture of both. Fresh sliced apples will bring out the fruity flavor. Fresh corn on the cob or canned corn will give the casserole a more crunchy texture.

*Pork with Rice and Peppers is an easy and tasty dish to prepare which is ideal for quick, filling family meals*

# Pork with Rice and Peppers

**6 pork cutlets**
**½ cup seasoned flour**
**¼ cup oil**
**1 onion, chopped**
**1 green pepper, seeded and cut in strips**
**1 sweet red pepper, seeded and cut in strips**
**1 clove garlic, crushed**
**½ cup water**
**salt and pepper**
**¾ cup long grain rice**
**¼ cup butter**

**1** Coat the pork cutlets in the seasoned flour. Heat the oil in a skillet and cook the cutlets for about 10 minutes until browned on both sides.

**2** Remove the cutlets and keep warm. Sauté the onion, green and red peppers and garlic until soft. Then return the cutlets to the pan and add the water and seasoning. Bring to a boil, then simmer, covered with a lid, for 20 minutes.

**3** Meanwhile, cook the rice in boiling salted water until tender. Drain and place in a buttered mold. Press it down firmly and unmold onto a serving dish.

**4** Surround the molded rice with the cutlets, peppers and onions and serve immediately.

*Serves 6*

**Tips:** You can use either pork chops or cutlets for this dish. It tastes especially delicious if served in a tomato sauce. Just add some skinned, seeded and chopped tomatoes, tomato paste, sliced mushrooms and a pinch of basil. For a special occasion, substitute white wine or dry sherry for the water.

1 Twelve hours or the night before the dish is required, prepare the marinade. Mix two pinches each of salt, pepper and paprika, and sprinkle it over the pork chops 2 Place the chops in a plastic bag and top each one with a bay leaf. Insert a sprig of thyme 3 Pour in half of the wine and the rum, holding the opening of the bag upright so that the liquid does not seep out 4 Seal the bag tightly and let the chops marinate overnight 5 Pour the other half of the wine over the prunes and let soak for 1 hour. Then place them in a saucepan, bring to a boil and simmer 15 minutes 6 Melt the oil and butter in a pan and coat the pork chops in flour. Sauté the chops a few minutes on each side to brown them 7 Pour the strained marinade over the chops. Cover the pan and simmer gently for 20 minutes 8 Transfer the chops to a heated serving dish 9 Simmering the pan juices over low heat, stir in the cream with a wooden spoon until well blended. Continue to cook for 5 minutes, stirring constantly 10 Strain the prunes and add them to the sauce. Taste, and add more salt and pepper if required. Stir and simmer for a few more minutes 11 To serve, arrange the prunes in the middle of the dish on top of the pork chops, and strain the sauce over the whole dish

# Pork Chops with Prunes

2 pinches each salt, pepper,
 paprika
4 pork chops
4 bay leaves
sprig thyme
1¼ cups dry white wine
¼ cup rum
2 cups prunes
2 tablespoons oil
2 tablespoons butter
¼ cup flour
¼ cup light cream

1 Prepare the marinade by mixing the salt, pepper and paprika and sprinkling it over both sides of the pork chops. Place the chops in a dish or plastic bag, top each one with a bay leaf, and add a sprig of thyme, half the wine and rum. Marinate for 12 hours or overnight.

2 Soak the prunes in the rest of the wine for an hour, then put them in a saucepan and bring to a boil. Simmer for 15 minutes and drain from the liquid.

3 Remove the pork chops from the marinade, and pat dry with a kitchen towel. Strain and reserve the marinade. Heat the oil and butter in a skillet. Coat the chops in flour and fry them for a few minutes on each side until just browned.

4 Pour the marinade over the chops, cover the pan and simmer over low heat for 20 minutes.

5 Remove the chops to a serving dish and keep warm. Stir the cream into the pan juices, and cook for 5 minutes at a gentle simmer. Add the prunes and stir for a few more minutes.

6 Strain the prunes from the sauce with a slotted spoon and arrange them in the middle of the serving dish on the chops. Strain the sauce over the whole dish and serve immediately, very hot.

*Serves 4*

# Pork Chops with Rhubarb

1 lb. rhubarb
¼ cup butter
4 large pork chops
2 tablespoons flour
salt and pepper
1 tablespoon honey
pinch of cinnamon
1 tablespoon chopped parsley

1 Thoroughly clean the rhubarb and cut it into chunks. Boil it for 5 minutes and drain.

2 Melt the butter in a large skillet. Dip the pork chops in the flour, seasoned with salt and pepper, and fry them gently in the butter until cooked through, turning once. Transfer them to a serving dish and keep warm.

3 Add the rhubarb to the meat juices in the pan, and stir in the honey and a pinch of cinnamon. Cook gently, stirring frequently, until the rhubarb is tender. Serve the pork and rhubarb together, each pork chop garnished with a little chopped parsley.

*Serves 4*

**Tip:** According to the sweetness of the rhubarb and your own taste, sweeten the rhubarb with more honey or sharpen it with a little lemon juice.

---

*Pork Chops with Rhubarb may sound strange but they taste absolutely delicious with a tart but fruity flavor*

# Pork Chops with Cider Cream Sauce

4 pork chops
2 tablespoons flour
salt and pepper
¼ cup butter
1 large onion, chopped
1½ cups sliced mushrooms
1¼ cups cider
¼ cup heavy cream
1 tablespoon chopped parsley

**1** Coat the pork chops in half the flour seasoned with salt and pepper. Melt the butter in a large skillet and fry the pork chops slowly until cooked through. Remove the chops from the pan and keep them warm.

**2** Add the onion to the meat cooking juices and sauté gently for 3 minutes.

**3** Stir in the mushrooms and cook for another 3 minutes.

**4** Stir in the rest of the flour and cook for 1 minute. Take the pan off the heat and stir in the cider to make a smooth sauce. Return the pan to the heat and stir for 1 minute.

**5** Over low heat, stir in the cream and season with salt and pepper. Heat to just below the boiling point. Pour the sauce over the pork chops, garnish with the chopped parsley, and serve at once.

*Serves 4*

*Pork Chops with Cider Cream Sauce — an impressive combination — enriched with thick cream and sliced mushrooms*

# Pork Chops à l'Orange

4 thick pork chops
1 onion, finely chopped
¼ cup butter
¼ cup oil
1 cup fresh breadcrumbs
salt and pepper
pinch dried sage
grated rind and juice 1 orange
2 tablespoons flour
1¼ cups chicken stock

**1** Cut a pocket in each pork chop by making a slit in the same direction as the bone, cutting from the fat side through to the bone.

**2** Sauté the chopped onion in half of the butter and oil for 5 minutes until softened but not browned.

**3** Stir in the breadcrumbs, salt and pepper to taste, sage, and the grated orange rind, so that the mixture absorbs the cooking fats and forms a thick paste. If necessary, remove from the heat and use the milk to bind the mixture.

**4** Preheat the oven to 325°F. Stuff ¼ of the breadcrumb mixture into each chop, securing if necessary with a wooden toothpick. Arrange the chops in an ovenproof dish and keep warm.

**5** Heat the rest of the butter and oil in the pan, scraping up any residue. Cook the flour for 1–2 minutes. Remove from the heat and stir in the stock and orange juice and bring to a boil, stirring all the time.

**6** Pour the thickened sauce over the chops, cover, and cook in the oven for 15 minutes. Serve with buttered green beans.

*Serves 4*

## Pork Chops with Brussels Sprouts

**6 tablespoons butter**
**1 large onion, chopped**
**1 cup long grain rice**
**2¼ cups water**
**1 teaspoon salt**
**1 lb. Brussels sprouts**
**salt and pepper**
**4 pork chops, about 6 ozs. each**
**1 teaspoon chopped parsley**

**1** Melt 2 tablespoons of the butter in a saucepan. Add the chopped onion and sauté lightly without browning.

**2** Add the rice, stir well and cook for 1 minute. Stir in the water and salt. Bring to a boil and stir once. Lower heat, cover and simmer for 15 minutes until the rice is tender and the liquid absorbed.

**3** Cook the Brussels sprouts in boiling salted water for about 8

*Pork Chops with Brussels Sprouts makes a colorful and nutritious dish which is served on a bed of rice*

minutes until cooked but still firm. Drain. Melt 2 tablespoons of the butter in a pan, add the drained Brussels sprouts, cover and cook very lightly for 10 minutes, shaking the pan occasionally.

**4** Melt the remaining butter in a skillet. Season the pork chops with salt and pepper and fry over medium heat for about 10 minutes on each side. Remove the chops to a warm serving dish. Add 2 tablespoons water to the juices in the pan, and bring to a boil, stirring.

**5** Arrange the rice and the Brussels sprouts around the chops and pour on the sauce. Sprinkle with chopped parsley and serve.

*Serves 4*

## Pork and Kidney Sauté with Wine

**1 tablespoon oil**
**1 tablespoon butter**
**salt and pepper**
**4 pork chops, ½ lb. each**
**1 pork or beef kidney**
**1 tablespoon flour**
**1 teaspoon beef extract**
**⅔ cup dry white wine**
**juice ½ lemon**

**1** Heat the oil and butter in a skillet. Season the chops and add to the pan, cover and sauté over low heat for 7 or 8 minutes on each side until cooked through. Remove the chops to a warm serving dish and keep them warm.

**2** Remove the fat and skin from the kidney, rinse well and slice thinly. Season with salt and pepper and roll in the flour. Add to the skillet, cover and cook lightly for 8 minutes. Ar-

490

range on the dish with the pork chops.

**3** Pour off the fat from the skillet, retaining the meat juices. Stir in the beef extract and wine, and boil for about 5 minutes until reduced by half. Add the lemon juice, season to taste and pour on the meat.

**4** Serve with sautéed or roast potatoes, sprinkled with chopped parsley.

*Serves 4*

## Crisp Pork Chops with Peaches

4 pork chops, $\frac{1}{2}$ lb. each
1 tablespoon flour, seasoned with pinch each salt, pepper, dry mustard

1 egg, lightly beaten
$\frac{3}{4}$ cup fresh breadcrumbs
$\frac{1}{4}$ cup oil
4 canned peach halves in syrup
1 teaspoon cornstarch
1 teaspoon prepared mustard
1 teaspoon vinegar
$\frac{1}{2}$ beef bouillon cube, dissolved in $\frac{2}{3}$ cup boiling water
pepper to taste

**1** Coat the pork chops with the seasoned flour. Dip into the beaten egg and then into the breadcrumbs, pressing them firmly onto the meat with a knife.

**2** Heat the oil in a skillet and fry the chops over low heat for 7 or 8 minutes on each side.

**3** Meanwhile, drain the peach halves, reserving the syrup. Mix together the cornstarch, prepared mustard, vinegar and 2 tablespoons

*Pork and Kidney Sauté with Wine will be everyone's favorite — it is quick to make and relatively inexpensive*

of the peach syrup in a small bowl. Bring the stock to a boil, stir in the cornstarch mixture and simmer for 2 minutes, stirring.

**4** Season to taste with pepper, add the peaches and simmer for 5 minutes.

**5** Arrange the pork chops on a warm serving dish with the peaches and pour on the sauce. Garnish with parsley.

*Serves 4*

### Applesauce
Give a lift to any pork dish with a tangy, fresh applesauce. Peel, core and slice 3 medium size cooking (green) apples, and place in a small pan with 2 tablespoons sugar and the juice of a lemon. Cover the pan and cook for 12-15 minutes, shaking the pan occasionally. When the apples are soft, mash them with a fork and serve either hot or cold.

# Pork Roasts

The following recipes show just how many ways there are of serving pork roast aside from the traditional applesauce.

## Pork with Pineapple

6 tablespoons butter
⅓ cup oil
2-lb. loin pork roast
salt and pepper

⅔ cup water
1 small pineapple, cut into chunks, or ½ lb. canned pineapple pieces, drained

For the Gravy:
1 tablespoon flour
⅓ cup water
2 tablespoons Worcestershire sauce
⅓ cup pineapple juice
1 tablespoon cornstarch

**1** Preheat the oven to 375°F. Melt the butter in a saucepan and combine it with the oil.

**2** Remove the backbone and all the rind from the pork itself. Season the meat with salt and pepper and

---

*Pork with Pineapple — crisp, roast pork with fresh or canned pineapple chunks in a delicious, golden gravy*

---

brush all over with half the butter and oil mixture. Place the pork on a rack in a roasting pan and roast in the oven for 1½ hours or until the meat is well cooked. Baste from time to time with the water, to ensure the meat does not dry out.

**3** Meanwhile, heat the remaining butter and oil in a pan and sauté the pineapple pieces for 3 minutes on both sides or until golden. Remove from the pan and keep warm.

**4** When the meat is cooked, prepare the gravy. Remove most of the fat from the meat juice. Add the flour and stir over a low heat for 3-4 minutes until browned. Add the water, Worcestershire sauce, and the pineapple juice. Bring to a boil and simmer for 5 minutes, stirring all the time. Thicken with the cornstarch mixed with a little water. Check the seasoning.

**5** Place the meat on a heated serving platter, surround it with the pineapple pieces and, just before serving, pour on the gravy.

*Serves 8*

## Braised Leg of Pork

3-lb. shoulder of pork
1¼ cups dry white wine
⅓ cup brandy
2 shallots, sliced
1 clove garlic, crushed
2 carrots, sliced
1 bay leaf
sprig thyme
sprig parsley
salt and pepper
2 tablespoons fat
½ cup brown breadcrumbs
¼ cup water
1 teaspoon cornstarch

**1** Preheat the oven to 450°F. Trim the pork all around. Remove all the rind and some of the fat.

**2** Place it in a large bowl and cover

it with the wine, brandy, shallots, garlic, carrots, bay leaf, thyme and parsley. Cover and marinate for 6 hours, turning it from time to time.

**3** Wipe it, season it to taste with salt and pepper and place it in a roasting pan. Add the fat and sear the meat in the oven for 30 minutes. Strain off any excess fat.

**4** Reduce the heat to 350°F. Add the vegetables and herbs and baste the meat with the marinating liquor from time to time, until it is cooked. The cooking time will depend on the weight of the leg. Allow at least 30 minutes per lb. When cooked, sprinkle the meat with the brown breadcrumbs.

**5** Strain the juices into a saucepan. Season, add the water and boil it for 5 minutes. If necessary, thicken with the cornstarch mixed with a little water. Serve the sauce in a gravy boat with the meat.

*Serves 8–10*

*Pork with Rosemary — an unusual way of serving a roast by pot-roasting in white wine with mushrooms and celery*

---

## Pork with Rosemary

2 lbs. lean boned shoulder or loin
  of pork
salt and pepper
$\frac{2}{3}$ cup butter
1 carrot, sliced
1 large onion, chopped
1 branch celery, diced
$\frac{3}{4}$ lb. mushrooms
$1\frac{1}{4}$ cups water
$\frac{2}{3}$ cup dry white wine
2 sprigs rosemary
1 clove garlic, crushed

**1** Preheat the oven to 375°F. Season the meat.

**2** Melt half of the butter in a flameproof casserole. Add the meat and brown it on all sides. Remove the casserole from the heat.

**3** In a separate pan melt the remaining butter. Add the carrot and sauté for 5 minutes. Add the onion and celery and sauté for a further 5 minutes. Finally add the mushrooms, cover and cook on low heat for 2 minutes.

**4** Pour the contents of the pan into the casserole. Add the water, wine, one rosemary sprig and the garlic. Check the seasoning. Cover and cook in the oven for $1\frac{1}{2}$ hours or until the meat is well cooked.

**5** Serve garnished with the second sprig of rosemary.

*Serves 6*

## Stuffed Pork with Eggplant

2½ lbs. boneless loin of pork, rind
  and some fat removed
salt and pepper
1 lb. onions, chopped
1 clove garlic, crushed
2 tablespoons oil
8 tomatoes, skinned, seeded and
  chopped
1 teaspoon chili powder
⅓ cup raisins
1 cup cooked rice
1 egg, beaten
⅔ cup dry white wine
⅔ cup stock
2 eggplants, peeled and sliced
¼ cup flour
oil for deep frying

**1** Preheat the oven to 375°F. Cut the pork almost in half lengthwise and season.

**2** Sauté the onions and garlic in the oil until soft. Add the tomatoes and chili powder and simmer for 5 minutes. Add the raisins.

**3** Blend half the tomato mixture with the rice and egg and place the stuffing on the pork. Fold over the meat and tie at intervals. Place in a roasting pan and cook in the oven for 1 hour.

**4** Pour out the fat which has collected in the roasting pan. Mix the remaining tomato mixture with the wine and stock and add to the pan. Return to the oven for 30 minutes or until the meat is cooked. Baste occasionally, adding more wine to the sauce if it becomes too thick.

**5** Meanwhile, soak the eggplants in salted water for 15 minutes, then drain and dry. Coat with the flour and deep fry until golden. Keep warm.

**6** Remove the string from the roast and place the meat in a serving dish. Pour the sauce around it and add the eggplant slices.

*Serves 6–8*

---

*Stuffed Pork with Eggplant. A tomato and chili mixture is used in both the sauce and the filling*

## Pork with Prune and Almond Stuffing

2 lbs. boned loin of pork, rind
  and some fat removed
salt and pepper
½ cup long grain rice

For the Stuffing:
¾ cup pitted prunes, cooked
½ cup slivered almonds
2 cups fresh breadcrumbs

For the Gravy:
1¼ cups stock
½ beef bouillon cube
1 teaspoon cornstarch
½ cup port or dry sherry (optional)

**1** Preheat the oven to 375°F.

**2** Spread the meat flat and season the inside. Combine the ingredients for the stuffing and place along the center of the meat. Roll up and secure with string. Season the outside of the meat and roast in the preheated oven for 1¼ hours, basting from time to time with a little water.

**3** Meanwhile, cook the rice in boiling salted water until tender. Drain and keep warm.

**4** Place the stock in a pan, crumble in the bouillon cube and bring to a boil. Add the cornstarch, mixed with a little water, and cook for a few minutes more. Season the gravy and add the port or sherry, if used.

**5** Place the rice on a serving dish and place the roast pork on the top. Serve with the gravy and applesauce.

*Serves 6*

**Tip:** You can substitute other nuts such as chopped walnuts for the almonds in the stuffing.

---

*Pork with Prune and Almond Stuffing, on a bed of rice, is served with a deliciously rich wine-flavored gravy*

# Look 'n Cook Crown Roast of Pork

1 Remove the backbones from the two pork loins
2 Cut 1½ inches of the fat from the ends of the bones
3 Trim away the sinew from between the bones
4 Bend the two cuts around to form the crown shape and secure with string 5 Place the crown in a roasting pan and brush all over with the melted butter 6 Wrap aluminum foil around the ends of the bones to prevent them from burning during the cooking 7 Heat the rest of the butter in a skillet, add the onion and celery and sauté until they are soft 8 Add the sausage meat and

cook until the fat runs out of the meat **9** Drain the excess fat from the pan **10** Add the breadcrumbs, rosemary, parsley, seasoning and stock and mix well **11** Place the stuffing mixture in the center of the crown and cover with a circle of aluminum foil to prevent drying out. Roast in the oven, allowing 30 minutes per lb. **12** Remove from the oven, discard the pieces of foil and place a cutlet cap on the end of each bone **13** Garnish roast with peas and roast potatoes and serve.

# Crown Roast of Pork

2 loins of pork, each containing 8 chops, (see page 496)
¼ cup melted butter
1 onion, finely chopped
2 branches celery, finely chopped
1 cup pork sausage meat
2 cups fresh breadcrumbs
1 teaspoon rosemary
2 tablespoons finely chopped parsley
½ teaspoon thyme
salt and pepper
¼ cup chicken stock

**1** Remove the backbone from the loins. Cut 1½ inches of the fat away from the ends of the bones. Trim away the sinew from between the bones.

**2** Bend the 2 loins around to form the crown and secure with string. Place the crown in a roasting pan and brush all over the outside with the melted butter. Wrap pieces of aluminum foil around the ends of the bones to prevent them from burning.

**3** Preheat the oven to 350°F. Prepare the stuffing: heat the remaining butter in a skillet, add the onion and celery and sauté until they are soft.

**4** Add the sausage meat and cook until all the fat has run out of the meat. Drain the excess fat from the pan.

**5** Stir in the breadcrumbs, rosemary, parsley, thyme, seasoning and stock and mix.

**6** Place the stuffing in the center of the crown and cover the stuffing with a circle of foil.

**7** Roast the crown in the oven, allowing 30 minutes per lb.

**8** Before serving, remove the pieces of foil and place a cutlet cap on the end of each bone. Serve the crown roast garnished with peas and roast potatoes.

*Serves 8*

# Loin of Pork
## Spanish-style

1 lb. navy beans, soaked overnight
2 cloves garlic, crushed
1 bay leaf
¼ cup olive oil
2 onions, sliced
2 lbs. boned loin of pork, cubed
½ lb. chorizo (spicy Spanish sausage) cut in ¾-inch slices
½ lb. smoked lean bacon, cut in small strips
3 tomatoes, skinned, seeded and chopped
1 tablespoon paprika
pinch saffron
4¼ cups boiling water
salt and pepper
2 cups green beans, trimmed and cut in 1½-inch lengths
small green cabbage, quartered
6 eggs

**1** Drain the navy beans, rinse and place in a pan. Cover with fresh cold water and add 1 clove of garlic and the bay leaf. Bring to a boil, reduce the heat and simmer for 1 hour.

**2** Heat the oil in a pan and add the onion, pork, chorizo, bacon, the remaining garlic and the tomatoes. Add the paprika and saffron and cook gently for 7 or 8 minutes, stirring constantly.

**3** Pour in the boiling water, season with salt and pepper and cook over low heat for 45 minutes.

**4** When the navy beans have cooked for 1 hour, drain and add them to the pork and simmer for 30 minutes more, or until tender.

**5** Add the green beans and cabbage and cook for 20 minutes.

**6** Meanwhile, cook the eggs in boiling water for 10 minutes, cover with cold water and then remove the shells.

**7** Transfer the pork mixture to a heated serving dish and garnish with the hard-boiled eggs. Serve very hot.

*Serves 6*

# Pork Orloff

¼ cup butter
few bacon pieces
3 lbs. loin of pork
1 onion
1 carrot, sliced
1 bay leaf
bouquet garni
salt and pepper
3 tablespoons grated Parmesan cheese
2 tablespoons butter, cut in pieces

For the Purée:
¼ cup butter
1 tablespoon oil
4 onions, chopped
1 lb. mushroom caps, diced
⅔ cup thick white sauce
⅔ cup heavy cream
pinch grated nutmeg
3 tablespoons grated Parmesan cheese

**1** Heat the butter in a pan, add the bacon and pork and cook until browned. Add the onion, sliced carrot, bay leaf, bouquet garni and seasoning and then cover with water. Cover the pan and cook slowly for 1¾ hours.

**2** Meanwhile, make the purée. Heat the butter and oil in a pan and sauté the chopped onion for 10 minutes, without browning. Add the diced mushrooms and cook for 1 minute.

**3** Strain off the fat and add the white sauce and cream. Mix well and season with salt, pepper and nutmeg. Stir in the cheese and cook for 3 minutes. Cool.

**4** Preheat the oven to 450°F. Lift the pork from the pan and carve it into thick slices. Spread each slice with purée and replace the slices to resemble the original roast.

**5** Cover with the remaining purée and sprinkle with the grated Parmesan cheese and the pieces of butter. Return to the oven for 5-10 minutes to brown.

*Serves 6–8*

# Loin of Pork with Cheese Glazing

2½ lbs. loin of pork, boned and
  derinded
salt and pepper
¾ lb. Gruyère cheese, diced
2½ cups fresh breadcrumbs
1 tablespoon Kirsch
1 tablespoon oil
1 cup beef stock
1 onion, quartered
2 branches celery, diced
1¼ cups dry white wine
1 teaspoon cornstarch
½ cup grated Cheddar cheese
1 teaspoon chopped celery leaves

**1** Preheat the oven to 375°F.

*Loin of Pork with Cheese Glazing
is stuffed with a rich Kirsch and
cheese mixture and glazed with
melted Cheddar*

**2** Make a slit along the pork and
season the inside. Prepare the stuffing: combine the Gruyère, breadcrumbs and Kirsch and place in the
center of the meat. Roll up the pork
and tie with string. Brush the outside with the oil and place on a rack
in a roasting pan. Bake in the preheated oven for 1¼ hours, basting
from time to time with the beef
stock.

**3** Twenty minutes before the end
of the cooking time, add the onion
and the celery and return the pan to

the oven for 10 minutes.

**4** Then add the wine and return the
pan to the oven for another 10 minutes.

**5** When the cooking time is up,
drain the gravy into a saucepan,
remove surplus fat and thicken with
the cornstarch mixed with a little
water. Season the gravy.

**6** Remove the string and sprinkle
meat with the grated Cheddar and
return to the oven for a few minutes
to melt the cheese. Serve with gravy
and sprinkled with the chopped
celery leaves.

*Serves 6–8*

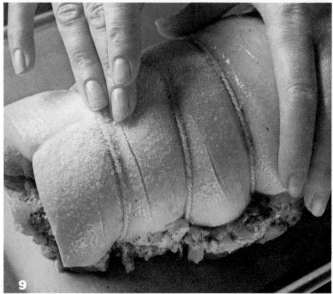

1 Score the rind of the boned pork with a sharp knife and set the roast aside 2 Peel and finely chop the onion 3 Sauté the onion in the butter over low heat until soft and lightly golden in color 4 Finely chop the apricots and walnuts and mix with the onion, breadcrumbs, parsley and salt and pepper to taste 5 Bind with the egg and mix well 6 Place the stuffing on the inner side of the meat and press it down well 7 Roll the meat up and tie it tightly with string 8 Brush the skin all over with the oil 9 Rub the skin well with salt to ensure a crisp crackling 10 Serve the stuffed pork with boiled, sliced leeks

## Pickled Pork with Saffron Rice

3 lbs. pork loin, boned
1 tablespoon saltpeter
1 lb. coarse salt
1 teaspoon ground ginger
salt and pepper
4 cloves
2 cups long grain rice
¼ teaspoon ground saffron
¼ cup butter

**1** Buy the pork loin the day before the dish is to be served. Rub saltpeter over it. Put a layer of coarse salt in an earthenware bowl. Lay in the meat and cover with the rest of the salt. Leave it for 24 hours in a cool place.

**2** Remove the pork from the salt, wash it thoroughly in cold water and dry it.

**3** Preheat the oven to 375°F. Spread out a cloth and put the meat onto it, fat side down. Sprinkle with the ginger and pepper to taste. Roll it up, seasoned side inside, tying it tightly with string.

**4** Using the point of a sharp knife, cut the fat in criss-cross lines forming a diamond pattern. Stud the meat with the 4 cloves and season with pepper.

**5** Pour ½ cup of warm water into a roasting pan with a rack. Place the meat on the rack and roast in the oven for about 1¼ hours or until cooked through.

**6** Put the rice into a pan with 5 cups cold water, the saffron and salt to taste. Cover and cook for 20 minutes, steaming covered off the heat until the rice is tender and the water absorbed. Add the butter, season with pepper and fluff up with a fork.

**7** Arrange the sliced pork on the rice to serve.

*Serves 8*

## Boned Blade of Pork with Apricot and Walnut Stuffing

4 lbs. blade or shoulder of pork, boned
1 onion, finely chopped
1 tablespoon butter
⅓ cup dried apricots, soaked in water overnight and finely chopped
12 walnut halves, finely chopped
1 cup fresh white breadcrumbs
1 tablespoon chopped parsley
salt and pepper
1 egg
1 tablespoon oil
1 teaspoon salt

**1** Preheat the oven to 450°F. Score the rind of the pork with a sharp knife.

**2** Sauté the onion gently in the butter until lightly golden.

**3** Mix together the apricots, walnuts, onion, breadcrumbs, parsley and salt and pepper to taste. Mix in the egg.

**4** Place the stuffing on the inner side of the meat. Roll up the meat and tie tightly with string. Place in a buttered roasting pan, brush with the oil and rub the salt into the skin.

**5** Roast for 30 minutes or until the surface has crackled. Turn the oven to 375°F and roast for another hour.

*Serves 6*

## Flemish Pork with Red Cabbage

2¼ lbs. pork loin
salt and pepper
pinch each cinnamon and coriander
¼ cup oil
1 small red cabbage, shredded
1 onion, chopped
1 clove garlic, finely chopped

½ cup vinegar
2 apples, peeled, cored and thinly sliced
1 tablespoon sugar
1 teaspoon chopped parsley
½ beef bouillon cube dissolved in 1¼ cups water
1 tablespoon tomato paste
2 teaspoons cornstarch, mixed with water

**1** Preheat the oven to 375°F. Remove the rind from the pork and season with salt, pepper and mixed spice. Brush with oil and place on a rack in a roasting pan. Roast in the preheated oven for 1¼ hours, basting frequently with 1 cup water.

**2** Place the cabbage in an earthenware bowl with the onion, garlic, vinegar and 2½ cups water. Let stand for 15 minutes.

**3** Add the apples to the cabbage with the sugar and seasoning. Transfer to a stainless steel pan, bring to a boil and simmer for 20 minutes.

**4** Transfer the pork to a serving dish. Surround with the cabbage in its liquid and sprinkle with parsley.

**5** Pour off the fat from the roasting pan, retaining the meat juices. Add the stock and tomato paste, bring to a boil and simmer for 5 minutes. Add the cornstarch to the pan and simmer for 1 minute, stirring. Season and strain into a sauce boat to serve.

*Serves 6*

**Tips:** To save time, instead of pickling a loin of pork, you can buy a ham. If you are not a lover of red cabbage, don't ignore this recipe. You can substitute green cabbage and omit the vinegar. However, if you do use red cabbage and want to make this dish extra special, use red wine instead of water.

*Flemish Pork with Red Cabbage is a delicious alternative to the usual roast with its spicy flavor*

# Pork Casseroles

Casseroles provide nourishing and inexpensive meals for cold winter evenings and pork provides just that extra special richness. Always remember that pork demands thorough cooking. To determine when the meat is cooked remove a piece from the casserole and slice it. The flesh should be white or greyish, never pink. The delicious recipes below show you just how many interesting ways there are to prepare pork in a casserole, both for the family and for guests on a special occasion.

## Pork Portuguese

2 lbs. lean pork, cut into cubes
¼ cup flour
salt and pepper
¼ cup oil
2 large onions, chopped
3 branches celery, coarsely diced
1 green pepper, seeded and cut into squares
2 large tomatoes, skinned, seeded and chopped
1¼ cups water
1¼ cups dry white wine
2 tablespoons tomato paste
1 clove garlic, crushed
bouquet garni

---

*Pork Piedmontese — zucchini filled with a liver and bacon stuffing and then surrounded by a hot pork casserole*

**1** Preheat the oven to 350°F. Roll the pork in the flour seasoned with salt and pepper. Shake off any excess.

**2** Heat the oil in a pan, add the meat, cover and brown for 10 minutes. Transfer to a casserole.

**3** In the same pan gently brown the chopped onions. Add the celery, pepper and tomatoes and cook over moderate heat for 5 more minutes. Transfer the vegetables to the casserole.

**4** Stir in the water, wine and tomato paste. Add the garlic and bouquet garni and season to taste.

**5** Cover and braise in the preheated oven for 1¼ hours or until the meat is tender.

**6** Serve with a bowl of piping hot savory rice.

*Serves 6*

## Pork Piedmontese

¼ cup oil
1½ lbs. lean pork, cut into cubes
2 tablespoons flour
1 tablespoon tomato paste
1¼ cups water
⅔ cup dry white wine
⅓ cup light cream
juice 1 lemon
pinch oregano
salt and pepper
3 medium zucchini

For the Stuffing:
¼ lb. calves liver
salt and pepper
2 tablespoons flour
2 tablespoons oil
1 onion, chopped
2 thin slices bacon
¾ cup mushrooms, finely sliced
1 tablespoon Parmesan cheese
¼ cup dry white wine
⅓ cup heavy cream

*Pork Portuguese, served with rice pilaf, is a tasty way of serving pork in white wine with tomatoes, celery and peppers*

**1** Preheat the oven to 350°F. Heat the oil in a pan. Add the meat and brown for 12 minutes. Sprinkle in the flour and stir. Cook for one minute, then add the tomato paste, water and wine. Bring to a boil and simmer for 15 minutes. Stir in the cream, lemon juice and oregano. Season and transfer to a casserole. Bake in the preheated oven for one hour or until the meat is tender.

**2** Meanwhile, cut the zucchini in half lengthwise. Cook them for 5 minutes in boiling salted water. Drain and keep warm.

**3** If necessary remove the membrane from the liver. Cut it into small cubes and roll in seasoned flour.

**4** In a separate pan, heat the oil. Add the onion and sauté until it is soft. Add the bacon, liver, mushrooms and Parmesan cheese and cook for 5 minutes on moderate heat. Pour in the wine and cream. Stir and simmer for a further 5 minutes. Check the seasoning.

**5** With a spoon scoop out the seeds from the zucchini halves. Place the zucchini on a warm serving dish and spoon the stuffing mixture into the cavities. Surround with the hot pork casserole and serve.

*Serves 6*

**Tips:** You can use this tasty stuffing for other vegetables besides zucchini. Try using it in eggplants or even red and green peppers. To give it an even richer, more distinctive flavor, substitute a fortified wine such as sherry or port for the white wine.

## Pork Paupiettes Braised in Beer

1 lb. lean loin of pork
salt and pepper
2 tablespoons fat
3 carrots
1 lb. small onions
$\frac{1}{4}$ cup flour
1 tablespoon tomato paste
$1\frac{2}{3}$ cups brown stock
$1\frac{1}{4}$ cups beer
bouquet garni

For the Stuffing:
2 tablespoons chopped onion
1 tablespoon oil
1 cup white breadcrumbs
1 teaspoon chopped parsley
pinch thyme
$\frac{1}{2}$ egg to bind
2 chopped apricots
4 chopped walnut halves
2 teaspoons butter

**1** Cut the meat across the grain into 4 thin slices and pound them. Trim to approximately 5 inches × 4 inches and chop the trimmings into small pieces. Season the meat slices.

**2** Prepare the stuffing. Sauté the onion in the oil until it is soft. Combine the onion with all the other ingredients and mix in the chopped pork trimmings. Spread a quarter of the stuffing down the center of each meat slice. Roll them up and tie with string.

**3** Heat the fat in a pan. Add the paupiettes and lightly brown them all over. Then add the carrots and onions and continue cooking until the meat is golden all over. Remove from the heat.

**4** Drain off the fat and pour 2 tablespoons into a clean pan. Add the flour and stir over low heat until you have a brown roux. Mix in the tomato paste and allow to cool. Boil the stock and add it to the pan with the beer. Bring the sauce to a boil, remove any scum, season and pour over the meat.

**5** Add the bouquet garni, cover and allow to simmer on low heat for 1-1$\frac{1}{2}$ hours.

**6** Remove the string and place the paupiettes on a warm serving dish. Surround with the vegetables and pour on the sauce.

*Serves 4*

## Pork Alentago

$1\frac{1}{2}$ lbs. lean pork tenderloin, boned
$\frac{3}{4}$ cup dry white wine
2 cloves garlic, crushed
2 bay leaves
1 teaspoon paprika
salt and pepper
2 slices bacon, diced
4 slices white bread
1 clove garlic, halved
2 tablespoons oil
10 ozs. cleaned mussels or clams

**1** Cut the pork into 1-inch cubes.

**2** Combine the wine, garlic, bay leaves and paprika in a bowl. Season with the salt and pepper and add the pork. Cover tightly with plastic wrap or foil and refrigerate for 24 hours.

**3** Fry the bacon in a heavy skillet until the fat runs out.

**4** Drain the pork cubes, dry them thoroughly and brown in the bacon fat. Cover and cook over very low heat for 30 minutes.

**5** Strain the marinade and add the liquid to the pan. Simmer uncovered for 20 minutes.

**6** Meanwhile, remove the crusts from the bread and rub with the garlic clove. Heat the oil in a pan and sauté the bread until it is brown. Place the bread slices in a shallow casserole and keep warm.

**7** Add the mussels or clams to the pork and marinade and cook thoroughly. Pour the pork and shellfish over the bread and serve.

*Serves 4*

## Pork Canton

$1\frac{1}{2}$ lbs. lean ground pork
$\frac{1}{2}$ cup chopped onions
salt and pepper
$\frac{1}{4}$ teapoon fresh gingerroot, minced
1 egg, beaten
2 tablespoons oil

For the Sauce:
$\frac{1}{2}$ cup chopped onion
2 branches celery, diced
2 tablespoons cornstarch
$\frac{1}{4}$ teaspoon fresh gingerroot, chopped
2 tablespoons sugar
1 tablespoon soy sauce
1 cup chicken stock
$\frac{1}{2}$ cup peach juice
$\frac{1}{4}$ cup vinegar
$\frac{1}{2}$ lb. canned peaches, drained and diced

**1** Combine the pork, onion, salt, pepper and ginger in a bowl. Bind with the beaten egg.

**2** Roll the ground mixture into balls approximately 1$\frac{1}{2}$ inches in diameter.

**3** Heat the oil in a skillet and cook the meatballs for about 10 minutes or until done. Remove the meat from the pan and drain well.

**4** Prepare the sauce. Drain all but 1 tablespoon of fat from the pan. Sauté the onion and celery in the fat until the onion is transparent.

**5** Combine the remaining ingredients, except the peaches, and pour into the pan. Stir and cook until the sauce is thick and clear.

**6** Finally, add the meatballs and diced peaches. Cover and simmer gently for 10 minutes to allow the sauce flavor to impregnate the meat. Serve with hot rice or noodles.

*Serves 6*

---

*Pork Paupiettes Braised in Beer are stuffed with fruit, nuts and herbs and cooked in a tasty, beer-flavored stock*

# Oriental Pork

## Sweet 'n Sour Pork

1 lb. pork tenderloin, cubed
2 tablespoons sherry
1 tablespoon soy sauce
¼ teaspoon sugar
¼-inch piece fresh gingerroot, grated
salt and pepper
4 branches celery, sliced
1 sweet red pepper, seeded and diced
8 scallions, cut into 2-inch pieces
¼ cucumber, cut into wedges
3 tablespoons oil
½ lb. pineapple chunks with juice
6 tablespoons cornstarch
¼ cup vinegar

½ cup sweet white wine
1 tablespoon brown sugar
oil for deep frying

**1** Mix the pork with the sherry, soy sauce, sugar and ginger. Add pepper to taste and mix well. Marinate for 30 minutes.

**2** Sauté the vegetables in the oil until soft but not brown. Drain the pineapple reserving the juice and add the chunks to the pan. Stir-fry for 2 minutes.

**3** Mix 2 tablespoons of the cornstarch with the vinegar, and stir into the pan with pineapple juice, wine and sugar. Season and simmer for 2 minutes, stirring.

**4** Heat the oil for deep frying. Remove the pork from the marinade and add the marinade to the sauce.

**5** Coat the pork in the remaining cornstarch and fry it in the hot oil.

---

*Pork and Bamboo Shoots. Sliced pork tenderloin stir-fried with onion and garlic in a pineapple and ginger sauce*

Drain well.

**6** Serve the pork on a bed of fried noodles with the sauce.

*Serves 4*

## Pork and Bamboo Shoots

3 tablespoons oil
1 onion, chopped
1 clove garlic, crushed
1 lb. pork tenderloin, thinly sliced
½ lb. bamboo shoots, thinly sliced
1 teaspoon cornstarch
½ teaspoon ground ginger
1 teaspoon soy sauce
½ teaspoon anchovy paste
⅔ cup pineapple juice
pepper

**1** Heat the oil in a skillet and sauté the onion and garlic until soft but not brown. Add the pork and stir-fry until browned.

**2** Add the bamboo shoots to the pan, cover and cook gently for 10 minutes.

**3** Mix the constarch, ginger, soy sauce and anchovy paste with enough pineapple juice to make a smooth paste. Add to the pan with the remaining juice and simmer gently, uncovered, for 15 minutes.

**4** Season with pepper and serve with rice.

*Serves 4*

---

*Sweet 'n Sour Pork — traditional Chinese Food, which is becoming increasingly popular in countries all over the world. Serve it on a bed of fried noodles, with fried rice, boiled noodles and chopped mangoes*

## Spareribs Tahiti

2 lbs. pork spareribs
½ cup vinegar
1¼ cups water
¾ cup catsup
¾ cup brown sugar
1½ teaspoons soy sauce
2 large pinches salt
3 tablespoons cornstarch
¼ cup water

**1** Preheat the oven to 325°F. Divide the meat into individual ribs. Pour the vinegar and water over them in a roasting pan and bake for 1 hour. Skim off any fat from the liquid, strain the liquid and reserve.

**2** Stir the catsup, brown sugar, soy sauce and salt into the cooking liquid. Mix the cornstarch with the 4 tablespoons of water and add to the liquid. Stir over heat to thicken.

**3** Pour the sauce over the spareribs and return them to the oven to bake for 30 minutes or until browned. Serve immediately with rice.

*Serves 4*

## Stir-fried Pork with Nuts

½ lb. pork tenderloin
4 small carrots, cut in matchstick strips
3 tablespoons oil
pinch salt
1 onion, thinly sliced
1 clove garlic, crushed
2 thin slices fresh gingerroot, peeled and finely chopped
½ red pepper, seeded and sliced
¼ cup blanched almonds or cashews
½ cup chicken stock
2 tablespoons soy sauce
1 tablespoon sherry
1½ tablespoons cornstarch

**1** Cut the pork into thin slices across the grain of the meat. Blanch the carrots in boiling water for 4 minutes, refresh in cold water and drain.

**2** Heat half the oil in a pan or wok. Add the pork and salt and stir-fry for 3 minutes. Remove the meat from the pan with a slotted spoon and keep warm.

**3** Heat the rest of the oil in the pan. Add the onion, garlic and ginger, and stir-fry for 1 minute. Then add the pepper, carrot and nuts and stir-fry for another minute. Add the stock, soy sauce and sherry, and bring to a boil, stirring.

**4** Lower the heat and return the pork to the pan. Cover and cook gently for about 5 minutes or until the pork is tender.

**5** Mix the cornstarch to a paste with a little water, and add until the sauce thickens. Serve at once.

*Serves 3*

## Pacific Pork

1½ lbs. pork tenderloin
¼ cup flour
2 tablespoons shortening or lard
1 cup pineapple juice
½ cup crushed canned pineapple
½ teaspoon each salt, pepper, ground ginger, allspice
1½ tablespoons cornstarch
2 tablespoons water

**1** Preheat the oven to 350°F. Cut the tenderloin into 6 pieces, and coat them with flour.

**2** Melt the fat in a skillet and brown the pork lightly. Transfer the pork to an ovenproof dish. Combine the pineapple juice and fruit, salt, pepper, ginger and all-spice. Pour the mixture over the meat and bake uncovered for 45 minutes or until the meat is tender.

**3** Remove the meat to a serving dish and keep warm. Pour the rest of the cooking liquid into the pan and thicken with the mixture of cornstarch and water. Pour the sauce over the meat and serve.

*Serves 6*

## Pork Vindaye

1 lb. spare ribs or blade of pork
2 onions
2 cloves garlic
1 sweet red pepper
2 tablespoons oil
2 teaspoons vinegar
1 tablespoon curry powder
2 teaspoons ground ginger
salt
1 cup water

**1** Cut the meat into large chunks or, if using spare rib chops, remove excess fat and cut them in half.

**2** Finely chop the onions and garlic. Seed the red pepper and chop. Mix these together with the oil and vinegar and pound to a paste with a pestle and mortar.

**3** Stir in the curry powder, ginger and a good pinch of salt. Coat the pieces of meat with this mixture and place them in a large saucepan. Pour in the water, cover, and simmer for 2 hours. Serve with golden rice — boiled with a pinch of turmeric to color it.

*Serves 4*

*Pork Vindaye — large chunks of pork cooked gently in a spicy curry-flavored coating until succulently tender*

# Saté

*This is a traditional Indonesian dish of small pork kebabs served with a spicy peanut sauce, always featured among the many accompaniments on an Indonesian table.*

1 lb. pork loin
¼ cup soy sauce
¼ cup sherry
1 clove garlic, crushed
1 thin slice fresh gingerroot, finely chopped
1 teaspoon curry powder
2 tablespoons oil
⅔ cup fresh peanuts, finely chopped
1 teaspoon honey
few drops chili sauce
1 teaspoon catsup
1 teaspoon lemon juice
¼ cup peanut butter
1 teaspoon cornstarch

**1** Cut the pork into 1¼-inch cubes.

Mix together the soy sauce, sherry, garlic, ginger, curry powder and oil, and marinate the pork pieces in this for 3 hours, basting from time to time.

**2** Strain the meat from the marinade and thread the pieces onto kebab skewers. Broil the kebabs, turning frequently, until browned on all sides.

**3** Meanwhile, pour the marinade into a saucepan and add the rest of the ingredients except the cornstarch. Heat gently, stirring to blend them into a smooth sauce. Thicken if required with the cornstarch mixed with a little water.

**4** Take the cooked pork from the kebab skewers. Arrange the meat around a heated serving dish, and pour the peanut sauce into the middle. Use toothpicks to dip the meat

*A traditional Indonesian Rice Table with the famous Saté (foreground), Indonesian Rice (center), jumbo shrimp, curried chicken and bean sprouts*

pieces into the sauce. Serve with Indonesian Rice.

*Serves 4*

# Indonesian Rice

½ cup long grain rice
pinch turmeric
2 tablespoons oil
⅓ cup fresh peanuts, skinned
1 teaspoon cumin seeds
1½ tablespoons shredded coconut
salt and pepper

**1** Boil the rice in salted water with a pinch of turmeric. Rinse and drain.

**2** Heat the oil in a skillet. Add the rice and stir-fry for 3 minutes. Add the other ingredients, stir well and fry for another 3 minutes.

*Serves 4*

# All about Sausages

1 *Gutsleberwurst*
2 *Sulzwurst*
3 *Bierwurst*
4 *Salami*
5 *Leberrotwurst*
6 *Aalrauchmettwurst*
7 *Chorizo*
8 *Peppered salami*

Sausages come in a wide variety of flavors and sizes. Most are based on ground pork. How many times have you stood in a delicatessen and gazed longingly at the colorful display of sausages and been tempted to buy, but, through ignorance of their names or cooking methods, turned away empty-handed? The wealth of choice is overwhelming. In this section, we show you how to cook sausages from the most humble link sausage to the more exotic varieties. There are ideas for serving hot and cold sausages in new exciting ways and also recipes for making your own at home.

The history of sausages goes back about 5,000 years. There is evidence that the Sumerians, Assyrians and ancient Greeks all ate sausages. The Romans were real sausage lovers and our own word "sausage" is, in fact, derived from a Latin word, *salsisium*. Sausages became very popular at Roman feasts and orgies but were later outlawed by the early Christian church. It was the Romans who introduced the black pudding (blood sausage) into their colony of Britain and, of course, it still survives today. Early sausages were much more tasty and spicy than the sausages of today. Among the ingredients were mixed herbs, peppercorns, pine nuts and cumin. However, even in those days there were some unscrupulous butchers who tried to substitute horsemeat for pork.

Sausages have remained popular through the centuries and today there are at least 500 different varieties. They are made on a worldwide scale, not only in Europe but also in the Middle East and even China. There are smoked sausages such as frankfurters and Viennas, dry sausages such as salami, chorizo and mortadella, as well as the uncooked pork and beef varieties we fry or broil until they are brown and sizzling.

Nowadays, most sausages are made not only of meat and fat, seasoned with salt, pepper and herbs, but also breadcrumbs stuffed into blanched intestines. With a new process, modern technology can now make a sort of artificial sausage skin.

The Germans and Italians are probably the world's biggest sausage producers and consumers. They use beer, spices, onions, aromatic herbs, garlic, kidneys and tongue in their sausages. The Germans claim that they alone produce 1,458 different sausages.

There are six classifications of sausages: fresh, smoked, cooked, dry, new conditioned, and cooked specialties.

## Storing Sausages
You can store salted and smoked varieties of sausages in the freezer for long periods of time. Sausages will keep in the refrigerator for a few days or may be stored in a cool place. As long as the air is cool, you can hang them up in the traditional way. But protect them from flies and other insects.

## Serving Sausages
Sausages are more versatile than most of us realize, and broiling or frying them for breakfast or a snack are not the only ways of serving them. In this section of *Look 'n Cook*, we show you how to casserole and stew them, and even make your own. Mustard is the traditional accompaniment for sausages and nowadays there are many varieties and blends to choose from. Mustard can flavor a sausage casserole as well as being spread along the tops of fried sausages. Homemade tomato and spicy barbecue sauces also go well with sausages, as does bottled catsup.

## Flavorings for Sausages
You can now buy sausages in all sorts of different shapes and flavors. If you plan to be really adventurous and make your own sausages, then there are many herbs and spices which you can use to vary the flavor. Apart from the obvious salt and pepper, you can use spices such as paprika, cayenne pepper and chili powder for a hot, spicy result. Mace, nutmeg, cloves, garlic, cinnamon and allspice can also be used. Many commercially produced and packaged sausages and link sausages now contain herbs. You can use nearly all herbs in sausage-making, particularly sage and thyme. Rosemary, parsley, basil, marjoram and sorrel can all be used. In addition to herbs and spices, you can also use wine and even brandy.

## Making your own Sausages
Making sausages is really a very simple business and far less complicated than it may sound. Of course it is easier to go to your local supermarket and buy a package off the shelf, but the homemade sort are far more tasty and very rewarding. Also, you have more freedom of choice in that you can choose your ingredients more selectively and blend in your favorite herbs, spices and flavorings for a really tasty result. You don't need any expensive equipment — a meat grinder, especially an electric one, can be helpful, but as long as you chop the ingredients finely you can make reasonable sausages.

Opposite are some of the attractive, delicious sausages you can buy in most delicatessens. Nowadays, many stores offer a wide range of home-produced and continental sausages at very reasonable prices so you can afford to be a little adventurous and try some to eat cold or cooked, in a variety of ways. The names are often difficult to pronounce but don't be put off by this. In the pictures on the following pages, we identify different sausages and give you some useful information on their flavor, cooking methods and serving. Using this, you will soon learn to recognize the different varieties.

*A selection of some popular sausages: top row, from left to right — salami la, a hard sausage that will keep well; mild liverwurst; and a delicate cervelas fine. Below, left to right — net covered land salami; zungenwurst with chunks of tongue; spicy negroni and coarse pork katenrauchwurst*

# Cold Sausages

The sausages which may be eaten cold constitute a large group, and many of its members are very well known and popular. They have all been cooked, either by being cured and smoked at very low temperatures, or by boiling.

These cooking processes preserve the meat so that the sausages may be kept for some time without deterioration — a week or more in a dry, airy, cool place.

Once they have been cut open it is safer to store them in a refrigerator. To serve, cut in thin slices with a sharp knife and remove the outer

*Salami and Corn Salad, a light and appetizing buffet dish. The presentation of cold meats is always important*

skin. Arrange the slices overlapping on a platter, or fold them into rolls and secure with toothpicks. Sausages may be cut straight across to make rounds, or diagonally to make oval slices. The thick sausages may also be diced.

## Salami and Corn Salad

1 lb. German and Italian
 salami, thinly sliced
4 small ears of corn
½ lb. cauliflower florets
1 sweet red pepper, cut in strips
½ cucumber, sliced
2 cups cocktail onions

**1** Arrange half of the salami slices, overlapping, around a dish. Roll up the remaining slices and arrange in an inner ring.

**2** Boil the corn in water for 8 minutes.

**3** Boil the cauliflower florets for 5 minutes only.

**4** Pile all the vegetables in the center of the salami.

*Serves 6*

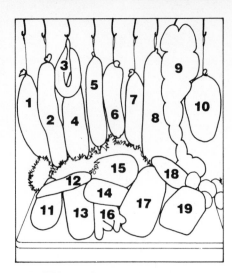

The sausages shown here have long been favorites in many countries and are now growing in popularity in this country. You may not find all of them in your supermarket deli department or neighborhood delicatessen. All of them are delicious.

**1** Salami La is a hard, spicy sausage which will keep for months.

**2** Leberrotwurst contains ground meat and bacon.

**3** Chorizo is a Spanish sausage flavored with red pepper.

**4** Salami Special is spicy, garlic flavored, and net-covered.

**5** Aalrauch Mettwurst has been smoked over fish bones.

**6** Gutsleberwurst is a coarse liver sausage, lightly seasoned.

**7** Haas Bauernsalami is one of the spiciest of salamis.

**8** Land Salami is mild, made of pork and beef with no garlic.

**9** Knackwurst may be cooked and served hot.

**10** Bierwurst is spicy, containing garlic and peppers.

**11** Cervelas Fine is mild and smooth, and will keep well.

**12** Negroni — a dry smoked sausage with peppercorns.

**13** Schinkenplockwurst is a sausage of smoked pickled pork.

**14** Liverwurst is mild and smooth textured.

**15** Schinken-sulzwurst contains mushrooms.

**16** Frankfurters may be reheated or served cold as canapés.

**17** Katenrauchwurst is made of pork smoked for a long time.

**18** Farmer's Salami is smoked dry and hard, with various spices.

**19** Pepper Salami has a peppercorn coating for extra flavor.

## Frankfurter and Potato Salad

3 lbs. new potatoes
salt and pepper
⅔ cup white wine
8 frankfurters, sliced
6 radishes
3 hard-boiled eggs, sliced
1 tablespoon chopped parsley

For the Dressing:
⅓ cup oil
3 tablespoons wine vinegar
1 teaspoon dry mustard
salt and pepper

**1** Boil the potatoes for 20 minutes in salted water. Drain and cut into cubes while still hot. Place in a salad bowl.

**2** Pour in the white wine immediately and toss gently. Add the frankfurters. Cool.

**3** Blend the oil, vinegar, mustard and seasoning in a watertight container. Shake well, pour over the salad and toss.

**4** Cut the radishes into flower shapes. Use the egg slices and radish flowers to decorate the salad, and garnish with the parsley.

*Serves 6*

## Cold Meat Platter

1 head lettuce
4 slices prosciutto ham

*Sausage snacks for any time: Chorizo Appetizers, front; juicy Hot Dogs on the right; and a Frankfurter and Potato Salad*

¼ lb. each of 4 different types of salami sausage
½ lb. marinated artichoke hearts, drained
2 tomatoes, sliced
1 red pepper, seeded and sliced
1 green pepper, seeded and sliced
5 anchovy fillets
¼ cup vinaigrette dressing
1 tablespoon chopped parsley

**1** Wash and thoroughly dry the lettuce leaves. Place half the leaves on a serving platter and shred the rest.

**2** Roll the slices of prosciutto into four bundles and place them across the center of the platter.

**3** Arrange the various sausage slices in a decorative fashion around the prosciutto. Place the shredded lettuce on either side of the platter.

**4** Serve with a bowl of artichoke hearts and a salad of tomatoes, peppers and anchovy fillets, tossed in a vinaigrette dressing and garnished with chopped parsley.

*Serves 6*

## Chorizo Appetizers

1 lb. 2 ozs. Spanish chorizo sausage
1 cup green olives, stuffed with pimiento
1 cup green olives, stuffed with almonds

**1** Slice the sausages into 24 pieces ½ inch thick. Place an olive with pimiento and one with almond on each of 24 toothpicks.

**2** Stick one toothpick into each piece of sausage and arrange on a large platter.

*Serves 8*

*A Cold Meat Platter can be made quickly and always looks delicious — just the thing to serve to unexpected guests*

518

# Making Sausages

Of course, anyone can buy ready-made sausages, but few realize just how easy they are to make at home and just how many exciting variations can be achieved, once you have the basic ingredients.

Making your own sausages is fun because you can experiment with all sorts of flavorings and seasonings — the combinations are literally endless. When making your own sausages, always be careful not to undercook them — this can lead to severe stomach pains and illness.

You can use virtually any kind of ground meat, but pork is ideal because of its high fat content, which enables the sausage to cook in its own juices and retain its distinctive flavor. The recipes below range from the simple pork sausage to a more exotic sausage flavored with herbs, spices and brandy. You will need only a meat grinder, a funnel, sausage casings (readily obtainable from the butcher) and a spare hour to create a really delicious treat for the family or friends.

Apart from the actual sausage meat, the procedure involved in all the recipes below is the same. Once you have prepared the meat, follow our instructions for a perfect sausage.

## Pork Sausages

1 cup breadcrumbs
¼ cup milk
1 lb. lean pork, ground
¼ lb. pork fat, ground
salt and pepper
pinch mace
pinch nutmeg
pinch ground coriander
1 egg, beaten

1 Soak the breadcrumbs in milk for 30 minutes. Drain them and squeeze out any excess moisture.

2 Blend the pork, fat, breadcrumbs, seasoning. Blend in the beaten egg and mince finely.

3 Stuff the mixture into the sausage casings.

*Makes 10-12 sausages*

---

## Brandy and Garlic Sausages

1 lb. lean pork
¼ lb. lean beef, ground
¼ cup brandy
1 cup breadcrumbs
1 tablespoon chopped parsley
2 cloves garlic, crushed
1 egg, beaten
1 teaspoon salt
pinch mace

### How to Make Sausages

1 Tie a knot in the end of one sausage casing. If you use a funnel place the other end over the neck of the spout and secure it with a piece of string.

2 Spoon the sausage meat into the funnel and force it through the spout into the skin. If you don't use a funnel be careful when stuffing the meat into the casing so that you do not rupture it.

3 With your hands, squeeze the meat to the bottom, forcing out any air bubbles in the process. Make sure that the skin is well packed.

4 When you have stuffed 4 inches of the casing, pinch it in so that no air remains in the sausage and twist it 5-6 times. Repeat this process until the casing is full and knot the other end.

5 These recipes will make between 10-12 sausages. You can make more by increasing the ingredients proportionally.

pinch black pepper
pinch paprika

1 Combine the pork and beef with the other ingredients.

2 Finely grind the mixture, and fill the sausage casings.

3 Hang the prepared sausages overnight in the refrigerator.

*Makes 10-12 sausages*

---

## English Sausages

1 lb. lean pork, finely ground
¾ lb. beef suet, finely ground
grated rind ½ lemon
pinch of thyme
pinch of marjoram
pinch of summer savory
½ teaspoon chopped sage
pinch of nutmeg
salt and pepper
½ beaten egg

1 Blend the pork, suet, lemon rind, herbs, nutmeg, salt and pepper.

2 Bind with the beaten egg and fill the sausage casings.

*Makes 10-12 sausages*

**Tip:** A novel alternative to the sausage casings is to cook the sausage meat in crêpes. Prepare a batter and make 12 crêpes. Mold the meat mixture into 12 narrow sausage shapes and wrap each one in a crêpe. Chill for 1 hour. When ready to cook, brush them with oil and bake for 15 minutes at 400°F.

---

*A sausage platter can be just as varied and delicious as a cheese platter. Arrange the sausages to contrast their shape and texture as shown here, clockwise from the left: frankfurters, leberrotwurst, gutsleberwurst, negroni, peppered salami, and salami la. Ideal accompanied by salad*

# Hot Sausages

Most of the pork sausages available to us on the market are delicious simmered, baked or broiled to serve hot.

They may be cut in chunks and added to soups and casseroles, chopped for sauces and stews, sliced for pizzas and quiches.

Allow $\frac{1}{4}$ lb. per person of freshly ground meat sausage or the smoked varieties, and slightly less for the spicier, drier types.

## Sausage and Vegetable Casserole

$\frac{1}{3}$ cup kidney beans, soaked overnight
$\frac{1}{4}$ small green cabbage, shredded
2 potatoes, peeled and sliced
2 carrots, scraped and chopped
1 large leek, sliced
2 onions, peeled and sliced
2 beef bouillon cubes dissolved in $3\frac{2}{3}$ cups boiling water
salt and pepper
1 lb. pork link sausages

1 Put the kidney beans into a large saucepan with the cabbage, pota-toes, carrots, leek, onion, stock and seasoning. Bring to a boil, reduce the heat and simmer for 1 hour or until beans are tender.

2 Twist each sausage into three, to make chains of three small sau-sages. Add to the casserole and sim-mer for a further 15 minutes, or until the sausages are cooked.

3 Serve with crusty bread.

*Serves 4*

---

*Sausage and Vegetable Casserole with juicy cabbage, carrots and beans makes a big, tasty meal just right for winter days*

## Pork Sausage with Sauerkraut

2 tablespoons cooking fat
1 onion, chopped
1 lb. sauerkraut

6 juniper berries
bouquet garni
salt and pepper
1 lb. smoked pork sausage, in one
  piece
½ chicken bouillon cube, dissolved
  in 1¼ cups boiling water
1 lb. baby carrots
2 tablespoons butter

**1** Preheat the oven to 350°F. Melt the fat in a pan and sauté the onion until soft but not brown.

**2** Wash and drain the sauerkraut and add to the onion, with the juniper berries, bouquet garni and seasoning. Stir over medium heat for 3 or 4 minutes. Turn into a casserole dish, place the whole sausage on top and pour on the stock.

**3** Cover the casserole and cook in the preheated oven for about 35 minutes, or until the sausage is heated through.

**4** Cook the carrots in boiling salted water for 15 minutes. Drain and toss in the butter.

**5** Remove the juniper berries and bouquet garni from the casserole. Arrange the sausage and sauerkraut on a heated serving dish, cut the sausage in thick slices and garnish with the baby carrots.

*Pork Sausage with Sauerkraut — the fatty content of the sausage is complemented by the crisp, acid sauerkraut*

*Serves 4*

**Tip:** The juniper berries give this dish a delicate gin flavor. If juniper berries are not available, add 1 tablespoon gin with the stock.

## Hot Dogs

6 frankfurter rolls
6 frankfurters
2 tablespoons strong prepared
  mustard
1 tablespoon tomato paste
2 teaspoons catsup

**1** Preheat the oven to 350°F.

**2** Split the rolls along one side and open them. Put them in the oven to warm through, but do not allow them to dry out.

**3** Place the franks in a pan of hot water and simmer gently for 10 minutes.

**4** Combine the mustard, tomato paste and catsup in a bowl and beat well.

**5** Spread the cut surfaces of the warm rolls with the mustard mixture, put a hot frankfurter inside each roll and serve immediately.

*Serves 6*

**Tip:** An excellent accompaniment to hot dogs is sliced, fried onion. And any hot spread or sauce can be used instead of mustard — try a spicy tomato or barbecue sauce.

---

**Pan-fried toasties**
Use your favorite spicy sausage for this quick and easy pan-fried sandwich. Butter 2 slices of white bread. Cover one slice with 1 oz. thinly sliced sausage, a little tomato relish and ¼ cup grated cheese. Fry it on both sides until the cheese is melted and the sandwich is golden-brown.

## Peas Pudding

1¼ cups dried split peas
1 onion
2 cloves
salt and pepper
¼ lb. butter

**1** Place the split peas in a bowl, cover with cold water and soak for 3 hours. Rinse thoroughly.

**2** Peel the onion and press a clove into each end. Place the onion and split peas in boiling water without salt added, and simmer for ¾-1 hour or until the peas are soft. Drain.

**3** Remove the cloves from the onion. Mash the peas and onion together or blend them in a blender to form a smooth purée. Season well, and beat in the butter. Serve hot with sausages.

*Serves 4*

---

*Sausages with Bean Purée shows how attractive sausages and pastry crescents can look, arranged in a wheel*

## Sausage Fondue with Dips

1 lb. cocktail sausages
½ lb. chicken breast, cut in strips
½ lb. cooked ham, diced
oil for deep frying
6 cups cooked rice
1¼ cups sliced mushrooms
¼ lb. pearl onions

For the Sausage Meatballs:
1 lb. pork and beef sausage meat
1 tablespoon chopped parsley
1 egg, beaten
1 onion, finely chopped
1 clove garlic, crushed
salt and pepper

For the Dips:
2 onions, chopped
2 tablespoons oil

---

¼ cup flour
1¼ cups stock
1 tablespoon curry powder
2 canned tomatoes
1 tablespoon vinegar
1 tablespoon brown sugar
grated rind and juice 1 orange
¼ cup red currant jelly
1 teaspoon prepared mustard

**1** To make the sausage meatballs, combine all the ingredients and form the mixture into balls.

**2** Arrange the meats on a platter around the fondue so that guests may spear pieces on fondue forks and cook them in the hot oil as long as desired. Serve with rice, sliced raw mushrooms and pearl onions, and a variety of dips.

**3** To make the dips, sauté the onion in the oil. Stir in the flour, then the stock, and season. Divide the sauce in 3 parts.

**4** To make the Curry Dip, add the curry powder to one part of sauce and blend thoroughly. Add the tomatoes, vinegar and brown sugar to the second part, and blend to make the Barbecue Dip. Blend the orange rind and juice, the red currant jelly and the mustard to the third for a Cumberland Dip.

*Serves 12*

---

## Sausages with Bean Purée

1½ lbs. of navy beans
2 onions
4 carrots
¼ lb. lean bacon
2 cloves
bouquet garni
salt and pepper
⅔ cup light cream
½ lb. frozen puff pastry, thawed
1 lb. pork and beef sausages
2 tablespoons oil

**1** Soak the beans in water overnight. Drain and place them in a saucepan, cover with water and boil for 45 minutes.

**2** Peel the onions and carrots and chop the bacon. Stud the onions with the cloves. Add the onions, carrots and bouquet garni to the beans and simmer for ½ hour or until the beans are tender.

---

*Sausage Fondue with Dips is an easy dish to prepare for a party, and will be popular with all the guests*

**3** Preheat the oven to 425°F.

**4** Remove the bouquet garni and cloves from the beans and drain them. Pass the beans, onion, carrot and bacon through a food mill or blender to form a smooth purée. Stir in the cream and season with salt and pepper. Transfer to a large serving dish.

**5** Roll out the pastry to ¼-inch thickness and use a 4-inch fluted pastry cutter to cut overlapping circles, making pastry crescents. Bake on a greased baking sheet for 15 minutes.

**6** Meanwhile broil the sausages or fry them in the oil until well browned. Arrange the sausages on the purée and place the crescents between them.

*Serves 4*

## Pan-fried Chorizo

1 lb. small new potatoes
½ lb. pearl onions
¼ cup oil
1 lb. Spanish chorizo sausage,
  sliced
2 cloves garlic, crushed
salt and pepper

**1** Peel or scrape the potatoes and blanch for 5 minutes in boiling water.

**2** Meanwhile, parboil the onions for 5 minutes.

**3** Heat the oil in a large skillet and fry the potatoes and onions for about 5 minutes until cooked and golden brown.

**4** Add the chorizo and garlic and fry gently for another 5 minutes.

**5** Season with salt and pepper and serve piping hot.

*Serves 4-6*

## Toad in the Hole

1 lb. pork sausages
2 eggs, beaten
pinch salt
⅔ cup water
⅔ cup milk
1 cup + 2 tablespoons flour
2 tablespoons sausage drippings

**1** Preheat the oven to 425°F.

**2** Place the sausages under a hot broiler and broil for about 5 minutes until they are beginning to brown.

**3** Meanwhile, make the batter for the Yorkshire Pudding. Place the beaten eggs in a bowl with a pinch of

---

*Pan-fried Chorizo is a simple but tempting mixture of spicy sausage, sweet new potatoes, and juicy onions*

salt. Add the water and milk, a little at a time, beating continuously.

**4** Sift the flour into another bowl and beat the batter liquid until the mixture is smooth.

**5** Place the sausage drippings in a small roasting pan in the oven.

**6** When the fat is hot, pour in half of the batter and bake for 20 minutes. Then place the sausages on top and cover with the remaining batter.

**7** Bake for a further 20 minutes until the batter is set, well risen and golden brown. Serve at once.

*Serves 4*

**Tip:** Another way to make Toad in the Hole is to place the sausages in the pan and pour all the batter over the top and cook until risen, crisp, and golden brown. You can substitute beef for pork sausages in this dish.

## Mortadella and Spinach

1⅓ cups dried lentils
1 onion, studded with 2 cloves
1 lb. whole mortadella sausage
2 lbs. spinach
¼ cup butter
salt and pepper

1 Soak the lentils in water overnight. Drain and place in a saucepan of water. Boil for 10 minutes. Remove the scum from the surface and, when the liquid is clear, add the onion and cook gently for 45 minutes until the lentils are tender.

2 Twenty minutes before the lentils are cooked, place the mortadella with them in the same pan, and heat it through.

3 Wash the spinach leaves, then boil covered for 5 minutes over low heat. Drain and squeeze out the surplus water. Mix in the butter and season. Arrange on a dish.

4 Slice the mortadella and place on

*Mortadella and Spinach with brown lentils is a nutritious meal, as well as a deliciously different taste*

the same dish as the spinach. Serve the cooked lentils separately.

*Serves 6*

## Somerset Sausage Casserole

¼ cup butter
1 lb. pork sausages
1 onion, sliced
2 apples, peeled, cored and sliced
⅔ cup cider
½ chicken bouillon cube
bouquet garni
pinch each coriander and cinnamon
salt and pepper

1 tablespoon tomato paste
2 teaspoons cornstarch
¼ cup water

1 Preheat the oven to 400°F.

2 Heat the butter in a flameproof casserole dish. Fry the sausages, onion and apple until the sausages are browned, and the onion and apple soft.

3 Add the cider and crumble in the bouillon cube. Bring to a boil, then add the bouquet garni, spices, seasoning and tomato paste.

4 Cover and bake in the oven for about 35 minutes.

5 Mix the cornstarch with the water and stir into the casserole on top of the stove, over heat, until the liquid thickens. Serve with baked potatoes topped with chives and sour cream. Sautéed slices of pumpkin and garden peas go well with this dish.

*Serves 4*

527

# Sausages and Pastry

Pastry makes a good accompaniment to sausages since it can stretch any dish to make it more economical and it can turn sausages into special party dishes when baked in golden flaky or puff pastry. There are, of course, classic sausage and pastry dishes, such as sausage rolls and in this section we feature another standard, Easter Pie, which is easy to make using our step-by-step guide.

## Dickens Pies

¼ lb. ground pork
½ lb. cooked pork sausages, skinned and chopped
2 eggs
¾ lb. puff pastry

**1** Preheat the oven to 425°F. Combine the pork, sausages and 1 egg.

**2** Roll out the pastry to ⅛-inch thickness and cut into twelve 3-inch rounds. Place a spoonful of the mixture in the center of 6. Roll the remaining rounds to enlarge them

*Sausage Pie is meaty and satisfying, and any leftovers will taste just as good when eaten cold the next day*

to 4 inches. Dampen the edges of the filled rounds with water and cover with the larger pieces. Press the edges to seal and place on a greased baking sheet. Brush with the remaining egg, beaten, and allow to rest for 20 minutes.

**3** Bake in the preheated oven for 20 minutes and serve hot or cold.

*Makes 12 pies*

## Sausage Cheese Flan

1 8-inch pie crust
½ lb. beef and pork link sausages
⅔ cup white sauce

2 eggs
salt and pepper
pinch cayenne pepper
½ cup grated Cheddar cheese

1  After making the pie crust, allow it to stand for 20 minutes.

2  Prick the sausages and broil them for 4 minutes to brown the outsides.

3  Preheat the oven to 425°F. Grease an 8-inch flan pan. Roll out the dough to ⅛ inch thickness and use it to line the flan pan. Prick the dough with a fork and bake empty in the preheated oven for 12 minutes. Cool. Reduce the oven temperature to 350°F.

4  Combine the white sauce and the eggs, season to taste and add half of the cheese. Pour the mixture into the flan and arrange the sausages on top. Sprinkle with the rest of the cheese and bake for 30 minutes.

*Serves 4*

*Sausage Cheese Flan combines hearty sausages with a light and tasty cheese mixture, to make a perfect supper*

## Sausage Pie

two 8-inch pie crusts
2 tablespoons shortening
½ lb. beef and pork link sausages
3 eggs
¼ lb. pork sausage meat
1 tablespoon chopped parsley
1 onion, chopped
3 tablespoons fresh white breadcrumbs
2 tablespoons brandy or sherry
salt and pepper
pinch paprika
pinch mace or nutmeg
pinch garlic salt

1  Preheat the oven to 375°F. Roll out the dough to ⅛-inch thickness and divide in two. Grease an 8-inch

pie plate with the shortening and line the bottom with one piece of the dough. Trim, and prick the base with a fork.

2  Broil the sausages for 3 minutes to brown the outsides. Cut into thick chunks and cool.

3  Beat 2 of the eggs and combine with the sausage meat, parsley, onion, breadcrumbs, brandy or sherry, salt, pepper, paprika, mace or nutmeg, and garlic salt. Blend in the chunks of sausage and place the mixture in the pie plate.

4  Cover with the remaining piece of dough. Beat the remaining egg and use to glaze the surface of the pie. Decorate with pastry trimmings and brush again with the beaten egg. Flute the edges of the pie with a fork to seal.

5  Bake in the preheated oven for 40 minutes and serve hot or cold.

*Serves 6*

529

# Sausage and Mushroom Pie

1 lb. pork sausages
¼ cup butter
2 onions, sliced
⅓ cup flour
1¼ cups milk
1¼ cups stock
salt and pepper
1 cup sliced mushrooms
¾ lb. puff pastry
1 egg, beaten

**1** Preheat the oven to 400°F.

**2** Prick the sausages and broil them until golden.

**3** Melt the butter in a pan and sauté the onions and mushrooms for 5 minutes. Stir in the flour and cook for 1 minute more.

**4** Gradually blend in the milk and stock and bring to a boil. Stir until thickened and then add the seasoning.

**5** Place the sausages in a pie plate and pour on the mushroom sauce. Roll out the puff pastry, cover the dish with it and trim off any excess pastry. Brush the top with the beaten egg and bake the pie for 40 minutes. Serve piping hot.

*Serves 6*

**Tip:** This pie can be stored in the freezer. Freeze it uncooked, and when ready to use, cook in an oven preheated to 425°F. for 45-50 minutes.

Vary the vegetables used in the sauce — try sweet corn, carrots or peas.

## Sausage Rolls

1 lb. pork sausage meat
1 lb. puff pastry
1 egg, beaten

*Sausage and Mushroom Pie holds a rich, chunky filling in a creamy sauce, topped with a light pastry shell*

**1** Preheat the oven to 425°F.

**2** Roll the sausage meat into a long strip 24 inches long.

**3** Roll out the pastry to ⅛-inch thickness and cut it into 2 strips 12 inches × 4 inches. Cut the sausage meat in half and place one half on each strip of pastry. Brush the edge of the pastry with beaten egg and fold over. Crimp the edge with a fork. Cut into pieces about 2½ inches long and brush with beaten egg.

**4** Place the rolls on a greased baking sheet and bake for 15 minutes. Serve hot.

*Makes 16 sausage rolls*

## Savory Bouchées

1 small onion, chopped
2 tablespoons oil
1 clove garlic, chopped
½ lb. pork sausage meat
¼ cup dry sherry
salt and pepper
1 tablespoon chopped parsley
1 lb. puff pastry
2 tablespoons shortening
1 egg, beaten
6 stuffed olives

**1** Preheat the oven to 425°F.

**2** Sauté the onion in the oil for 3 minutes. Add the garlic and meat and cook for 15 minutes, covered with a lid. Add the sherry, seasoning and parsley and keep the mix-

530

*Sausage Rolls, left, and Savory Bouchées, right, are ideal party dishes, tasty and neat for eating with your fingers*

ture hot while making the bouchée cases.

**3** Roll out the pastry to ⅛-inch thickness. Cut 12 rounds using a 2½-inch cutter. Grease a baking sheet with the shortening and place 6 rounds on the sheet. Press a 1½-inch cutter into the center of the remaining rounds to give 6 rings. Dampen the edge of the rounds with water and place the rings on top. Press together to seal. Brush the tops with the beaten egg and bake in the oven for 15 minutes until golden and puffy.

**4** Fill the bouchées with the sausage mixture, top each one with a stuffed olive and serve hot.

*Makes 6*

## Easter Pie

4 cups flour
9 eggs
½ lb. butter, softened
1½ lbs. pork sausage meat
1 tablespoon chopped parsley
½ teaspoon salt
pinch freshly ground black pepper
1 teaspoon mixed mace and
  coriander
pinch cayenne pepper
1 egg yolk, beaten
2 tablespoons shortening

**1** Form the flour into a ring on the work surface. Break in 2 eggs and add the softened butter. Mix together with the fingers, adding 1-2 tablespoons water, and knead the dough for 2-3 minutes until smooth. Roll the dough into a ball and place it in a cool place or in the refrigerator for 30 minutes.

**2** Cook 5 of the eggs in boiling water for 10 minutes, drain and cover them with cold water to cool.

**3** In a bowl, combine the sausage meat with 2 of the eggs and the parsley, salt, pepper, mixed spice and cayenne. Mix well.

**4** Shell the hard-boiled eggs to prevent them from discoloring; cover them with cold water until needed.

**5** Halve the dough and roll out each piece to a rectangle about ¼ inch thick.

**6** Place half of the meat mixture along the center of one piece of dough and arrange the hard-boiled eggs along the top of the meat. Cover the eggs with the rest of the meat mixture, making sure the eggs are well covered at the sides.

**7** Brush the border of dough around the meat with the egg yolk and place the second piece of dough over the top. Trim off the excess dough and crimp the edges of the parcel with the fingers to seal. Pinch together at intervals to produce a fluted edge. Preheat the oven to 350°F.

**8** Brush the whole parcel with more egg yolk. Roll out the dough trimmings to ⅛ inch thickness and cut out decorative leaf shapes. Arrange some into roses and place the roses and the leaves on the top of the Easter Pie. Brush the decorations with more beaten egg yolk.

**9** Grease a baking sheet with the shortening and place the pie on the sheet. Bake in the preheated oven for 1 hour. Allow to cool and decorate with sprigs of parsley. Serve cold.

*Serves 8*

# Look 'n Cook Easter Pie

**1** The ingredients **2** Form the flour into a continuous ring on the work surface. Break in 2 of the eggs **3** Add the softened butter and a little water and mix with the fingers. Knead the dough for 2-3 minutes until smooth.

Roll the dough into a ball and place it in the refrigerator for 30 minutes. Meanwhile, cook 5 of the eggs in boiling water for 10 minutes. Drain and cover with cold water to cool **4** Combine the sausage meat, 2 of the eggs,

parsley, salt, pepper, mixed spice and cayenne **5** Mix
the ingredients well **6** Shell the eggs and, to prevent
them from discoloring, cover them with cold water until needed **7** Cut the dough in half and roll out each
piece into a rectangle $\frac{1}{2}$ inch thick **8** Place half of the
meat mixture along the center of one piece of dough
**9** Arrange the hard-boiled eggs in a row along the top
of the meat **10** Cover with the rest of the sausage meat

# Look 'n Cook Easter Pie continued

mixture, making sure that the eggs are well covered at the sides **11** Brush the border continued dough around the meat with the beaten egg yolk **12** Cover the meat with the second piece of dough **13** Trim the edges of the dough with a knife **14** and **15** Crimp the edges with the fingers to seal and then pinch the dough together at

534

intervals to produce a fluted edge **16** Brush all over the outside of the pie with the egg yolk **17** Roll out the dough trimmings to $\frac{1}{8}$ inch thickness and cut out decorative leaf shapes. Form some of the leaves into roses and arrange the roses and leaves on the top of the pie. Brush with egg yolk **18** Bake the pie for 1 hour and then cool. Transfer to a serving dish and decorate the dish with sprigs of parsley. Serve cold

# Blood Pudding

Blood pudding is a boiled sausage consisting of pork blood, cereals and suet in a casing of pork intestine. It is the coagulation of the blood during the cooking which gives the pudding its characteristic color. Blood pudding is generally sliced, then fried or broiled.

*Blood Pudding Pilaf is a colorful mixture, with the richness of the pudding set off by the mild, fluffy rice*

## Blood Pudding Pilaf

1 cup long grain rice
$\frac{1}{3}$ cup oil
1 large onion, chopped
1 sweet red pepper, chopped
1 green pepper, chopped
3 tomatoes, skinned, seeded and chopped
$\frac{1}{2}$ lb. sliced mushroom caps
$\frac{1}{2}$ lb. blood pudding or Spanish chorizo, sliced
1 whole tomato, quartered

For the Dressing:
3 tablespoons oil
1 tablespoon vinegar
1 teaspoon prepared mustard
salt and pepper

**1** Boil the rice for 20 minutes, rinse and drain.

**2** Heat $\frac{2}{3}$ of the oil and sauté the onion until soft. Add the rice, stir and cook for 4 minutes, without coloring. Cool. Blend in the peppers, tomatoes and mushrooms.

**3** Fry the sliced sausage in the rest of the oil for 5 minutes. Cool.

**4** Place the sausages around the edge of a dish and pile the pilaf in the center. Place the oil, vinegar, mustard and seasoning in an airtight container and shake to mix. Sprinkle the dressing over the pilaf. Garnish with the tomato quarters and serve.

*Serves 6*

## Mixed Fried Sausages

$\frac{1}{4}$ cup bacon fat
4 herb pork sausages
3 frankfurters, halved lengthwise
3 German sausages, sliced
4 slices blood pudding
$1\frac{1}{2}$ cups sliced cold boiled potatoes
2 tomatoes, halved
salt and pepper
sprig watercress

**1** Heat the bacon fat in a pan and fry the pork sausages, covered with a lid, for 5 minutes. Remove from the pan and fry the frankfurters for 3 minutes. Remove and add the German sausages and the blood pudding and fry for a further 4 minutes. Keep the cooked sausages hot.

**2** Add the potato to the bacon fat and toss until golden. Add to the sausages. Sauté the tomato halves for 2 minutes and season to taste. Add the tomatoes to the dish, garnish with the sprig of watercress and serve.

*Serves 4*

*A plate of Mixed Fried Sausages. Clockwise from bottom: German sausage, blood pudding, herb pork sausages, frankfurters*

## Blood Pudding with Apple

1 lb. potatoes, peeled
3 large cooking apples
3 tablespoons oil
1 tablespoon butter
1 lb. blood pudding, sliced
1 teaspoon chopped parsley

**1** Boil and mash the potatoes and keep them warm.

**2** Peel and core the apples and cut each into 6 wedges. Heat half the oil and all the butter in a pan. Add the apple, cover and cook for 5 minutes on low heat until tender and golden. Drain and keep warm.

**3** In a separate pan, heat the remaining oil and add the sliced blood pudding. Fry on both sides until it is slightly crisp and heated through. Remove and drain.

**4** Place the mashed potato in the center of a heated serving dish and surround it with alternate portions of blood pudding and apple. Garnish the potato with the chopped parsley.

*Serves 4*

*Blood Pudding with Apple makes a deliciously cheap meal for the family and is especially good for a late morning brunch*

## Blood Pudding Casserole

$\frac{1}{2}$ cup oil
2 onions, sliced
$\frac{1}{4}$ lb. lean ham, cubed
2 tomatoes, skinned, seeded and coarsely chopped
2 branches celery, diced
1 clove garlic, chopped
$\frac{1}{2}$ lb. sliced mushrooms
salt and pepper
1$\frac{1}{2}$ lbs. blood pudding
1 tablespoon chopped parsley

**1** Preheat the oven to 350°F. Heat half the oil in a skillet. Add the onions and sauté until they are soft and slightly brown. Add the diced ham and sauté for 2 more minutes. Stir in the tomatoes, celery, chopped garlic and mushrooms. Season to taste, cover and cook over low heat for 5 minutes.

**2** Transfer the mixture to a casserole dish.

**3** Cut the blood pudding diagonally into slices $\frac{1}{2}$ inch thick. In the same skillet, heat the remaining oil and sauté the blood pudding slices on both sides for 1 minute.

**4** Add the blood pudding to the casserole and bake in the oven for 10-12 minutes. Garnish with the chopped parsley and serve.

*Serves 4*

**Tip:** Blood pudding needs very little cooking time. Whenever you include it in a casserole, make sure all the other ingredients are almost cooked before adding the pudding.

### Blood Pudding Fritters
Make a batter by blending 1 cup + 2 tablespoons self-rising flour, salt and pepper, 1 egg and $\frac{2}{3}$ cup milk in a bowl, until you have a smooth batter. Cut 2 blood puddings in half and slice each piece lengthwise. Dip each piece in the batter and deep-fry in sizzling oil until they are crisp and golden. This is a delicious treat for a family supper when served with catsup, assorted chutneys or mustard.

# Sausage Medley

Sausage dishes are among the cheapest and easiest meat-based dishes to prepare.

## Sausage and Chicken with Sauerkraut

½ lb. slab bacon
bouquet garni
1 onion, studded with 1 clove

4 chicken pieces
1 tablespoon butter
salt and pepper
1 lb. sauerkraut, drained
2 European sausages
4 frankfurters
⅔ cup dry white wine
1 lb. small new potatoes

**1** Place the bacon slab in a large saucepan, cover with water, add the bouquet garni and onion and simmer gently for 1 hour.

**2** Preheat the oven to 375°F. Brush the chicken pieces with butter, season and bake for 30 minutes or until cooked. Keep the chicken pieces warm.

*Sausage and Chicken with Sauerkraut is a popular German dish — it is filling and economical and easy to prepare*

**3** Drain the bacon slab, reserving the liquid, and place it in a flameproof casserole dish. Add the sauerkraut, continental sausages and frankfurters. Pour in the wine, cover and simmer for 20 minutes.

**4** Meanwhile, boil the potatoes for 20 minutes in the reserved water. Add more water if necessary.

**5** Drain and separate all the ingredients in the casserole. Slice the bacon into 4 thick pieces.

**6** Place the sauerkraut on a large warm serving dish. Arrange the frankfurters, bacon slices and chicken pieces on top. Place the potatoes and sausages around the rim and serve immediately.

*Serves 4*

## Frankfurters Baked with Cheese and Apples

2 tablespoons butter
8 frankfurters
2 teaspoons prepared mustard
3 cooked apples, peeled, cored and sliced
¼ cup brown sugar
¼ cup grated cheese
½ cup breadcrumbs

**1** Preheat the oven to 350°F. Butter a baking dish and place the frankfurters in it, side by side.

**2** Spread them with mustard and cover with the sliced apples. Sprinkle with the sugar and bake for 20 minutes. Remove from the oven.

**3** Combine the cheese, breadcrumbs and remaining butter and sprinkle this mixture over the top. Place the tray under the broiler until the cheese is bubbling and the breadcrumbs crisp.

*Serves 4*

## Sausage Kebabs Romana

½ lb. pork or chicken liver
1 tablespoon Worcestershire sauce
⅔ cup Marsala
1 tablespoon oil
1 clove garlic, finely chopped
¼ teaspoon oregano
pinch each salt and pepper
¾ lb. pork link sausages

**1** Skin the pork liver and cut into 8 chunky pieces.

**2** Mix the Worcestershire sauce, Marsala, oil, garlic, oregano and seasoning. Add the liver and marinate for 20 minutes.

**3** Thread 3 sausages and 2 cubes of liver on each of 4 long skewers.

**4** Place the skewers on a broiler pan and brush liberally with the marinade. Broil for 8 minutes, turning and brushing frequently with the marinade.

**5** Serve the kebabs with sautéed potatoes, garnished with parsley.

*Serves 4*

---

## Sausage Veal Roll

2 lbs. fresh leaf spinach
3 lbs. breast of veal
salt and pepper
pinch nutmeg
1 egg, beaten
1 cup fresh white breadcrumbs
1 lb. garlic sausage
2 tablespoons oil
1 beef bouillon cube, dissolved in 1¼ cups boiling water
⅔ cup Marsala wine

---

*Sausage Kebabs Romana is a meaty mixture of liver marinated in wine and Worcestershire sauce, cooked with sausages*

1 tablespoon tomato paste
⅓ cup heavy cream

**1** Preheat the oven to 400°F. Wash the spinach well and strip off the stalks. Place in a pan, cover and cook over medium heat for 5 minutes. It is not necessary to use any water as long as the pan is shaken regularly. Drain the spinach in a colander and press it well to remove all the moisture.

**2** Bone the breast of veal, lay it boned side up and season well. Place the spinach leaves on top and sprinkle with nutmeg and seasoning.

**3** Mix together the beaten egg and breadcrumbs and spread over the spinach.

**4** Skin the garlic sausage, place it on top of the meat and roll it up, tying it securely with string. Brush the outside with oil and season well.

**5** Place in a roasting pan and roast in the preheated oven for 1 hour, basting frequently with the beef stock.

*Sausage Veal Roll is unusual and a spectacular way of cooking garlic sausage inside a tender, mild breast of veal*

**6** Remove the strings from the cooked roll and pour the stock and juices from the roasting pan into a saucepan. Add the Marsala and tomato paste and boil for 5 minutes, then add the cream and boil for a further 3 minutes. Season to taste, and pour into a sauce boat.

**7** Cut the roll in thick slices and serve with the Marsala sauce and roast potatoes.

*Serves 8*

## Devilled Pork Sausages

1 lb. pork sausages
2 tablespoons oil
1 onion, chopped
2 tablespoons flour
1 cup peeled tomatoes
½ cup corn
¼ teaspoon sugar
dash Worcestershire sauce

**1 teaspoon prepared mustard
salt and pepper**

**1** Brown the sausages in the hot oil. Remove from the pan.

**2** Sauté the onion lightly. Stir in the flour and cook for 1 minute.

**3** Add the tomatoes and bring to a boil, stirring. Add the remaining ingredients with the sausages, cover and simmer for 30 minutes.

*Serves 4*

## Sausage Rolls with Cumberland Sauce

1 lb. pork sausage meat
1 tablespoon flour, seasoned with
 salt and pepper
8 slices lean bacon
2 tablespoons oil
2 oranges
1 teaspoon dry mustard
1 tablespoon brown sugar
pinch of salt
pinch of cayenne
pinch ground cloves
$1\frac{1}{2}$ cups red wine
2 tablespoons cornstarch
2 tablespoons lemon juice

1 Preheat the oven to 375°F. Form the sausage meat into 8 sausage shapes. Toss them in the seasoned flour. Roll a bacon slice around each sausage and secure with a wooden toothpick.

2 Heat the oil in a roasting pan. Add the sausage rolls and bake for 30 minutes, turning the rolls occasionally.

3 Peel one of the oranges with a potato peeler and cut the peel into matchstick-size strips. Put them in a pan with the mustard, sugar, salt, spices and wine. Bring to a boil. Cover and simmer for 8 minutes.

4 Mix the cornstarch to a smooth paste with the lemon juice, add the juice of 1 orange and stir into the sauce. Simmer for 2 minutes, stirring.

5 Peel the remaining orange with a sharp knife, removing all the pith, and slice into rounds.

6 Drain the cooked sausage rolls, removing the toothpicks and arrange them on a heated serving dish. Pour on a little of the sauce. Garnish with the orange slices. Serve the remaining sauce separately.

*Serves 4*

**Tip:** For a pleasant herby flavor, add 2 teaspoons chopped fresh sage or 1 teaspoon dried sage to the sausage meat before shaping.

*Sausage Rolls with Cumberland Sauce — the mild flavor of the sausage goes well with the wine and orange sauce*

## Salami Hotpot

two $\frac{1}{2}$-lb. salami sausages
$\frac{1}{2}$-lb. piece smoked slab bacon
3 medium onions
3 cloves
bouquet garni
2 bay leaves
3 lbs. small potatoes
$1\frac{1}{4}$ cups dry white wine
salt and pepper

1 Place the two whole salamis in a pan with the bacon, onions studded with the cloves, bouquet garni, bay leaves and $3\frac{3}{4}$ cups water.

2 Bring to a boil and simmer for 40 minutes. Skim.

3 Add the peeled potatoes, wine and seasoning to the pan and simmer for a further 30 minutes, or until the potatoes are cooked.

4 Cut the salami into chunks to serve.

*Serves 6*

*Salami Hotpot — a tasty mixture of salami, bacon and potatoes cooked in one pan — is a filling, yet economical dish*

# Spicy Mexican Rice

¼ cup butter
½ lb. frankfurters
½ lb. pork link sausages
1 large onion, chopped
½ sweet red pepper, seeded and finely chopped
½ green pepper, seeded and finely chopped
¾ cup long grain rice
chili powder to taste
1 chicken bouillon cube, dissolved in 1¾ cups boiling water
1 tablespoon tomato paste
½ cup sweet corn, drained
salt and black pepper
2 tomatoes
1 teaspoon chopped chives

1 Melt the butter in a large skillet. Fry the frankfurters and link sausages over medium heat for 4 or 5 minutes, shaking the pan to prevent sticking. Remove the sausages from the pan with a slotted spoon and cut them into chunky pieces.

2 Add the onion and peppers to the pan and sauté until the onions are lightly golden.

3 Add the rice and chili powder and cook over gentle heat for 2 or 3 minutes, stirring.

4 Stir in the stock, tomato paste,

---

*Spicy Mexican Rice gives frankfurters and link sausages the warm and exotic flavor of Mexico*

sweet corn, sausage pieces and seasoning. Bring to a boil, stir well, cover and simmer gently for 15 minutes, until the rice is tender and the liquid absorbed.

5 Cut the tomatoes into wedges and add to the pan for the last 5 minutes of cooking.

6 Sprinkle with the chives and serve.

*Serves 4*

**Tip:** To vary this dish, try replacing the chili powder with fresh chilies, which should be seeded and chopped and added with the onion.

# All about Ham and Bacon

*Ham steaks with pineapple*

Who could resist a delicious pearly pink, succulent ham as in our cover picture? In this volume we deal with ham, ham shank and bacon and give you exciting recipes for all three. But first we must distinguish between them.

Both the shank and ham come from the hind leg of the pig, whereas bacon comes from the body. Ham is removed from the hind leg before salting and is then cured. Some hams such as Parma ham (prosciutto) are smoked and then eaten raw. Bacon is the salted flesh which may be smoked or unsmoked. Smoked bacon keeps longer than the unsmoked types.

## Choosing Ham and Bacon

When buying cooked sliced ham, it should have pink-colored flesh and very white fat. Make sure that it is moist and not dried out. Bacon should smell pleasant and have firm white fat and pink lean flesh. If unsmoked, the rind should be pale and creamy; if smoked, a golden-brown.

## Storing Bacon and Ham

Store bacon and ham in a refrigerator. Always wrap it in foil or plastic wrap to keep it fresh. Wax paper is not very satisfactory as it will allow the bacon to dry out. You can store bacon and ham for up to a week in the refrigerator. You can, of course, freeze it.

## Types of Ham

There are many different types and varieties of ham which you can buy, both imported and home-produced. You can buy country hams such as the Virginia and Kentucky varieties. These may be cured in many ways. Of course, there are also the smoked hams which are thinly sliced and eaten raw such as the famous Italian Parma ham (prosciutto) and the French Bayonne ham, which is salted and smoked with herbs.

**Glazes for Fresh Hams:** Your ham will taste even more delicious if you make a glaze for it. Boil the ham for half the cooking time, then bake in the oven and, half an hour before removing the ham, score the fat in a diamond pattern. Stud each diamond with a clove and baste with a glaze. You can make a glaze with a little honey mixed with orange juice and grated rind or pineapple juice and brown sugar. You can even add some wine or cider and spices such as ginger, allspice or ground cloves. Maple syrup or honey mixed with spices makes a sweeter alternative.

## Cuts of Bacon

These tend to vary and may be either smoked or unsmoked. Although most people tend to associate bacon slices with breakfast-time and the delicious aroma of sizzling bacon wafting around the house, bacon can be served in a variety of ways and in different dishes. It can be fried, broiled, roasted or boiled depending on the cut. The breakfast slices are back, streaky or middle cut, all of which may be smoked or fresh. Back is the leanest, streaky is streaked through with fat, while middle cuts consist of long slices of streaky and back combined. Collar and hock are the most common cuts of bacon. They tend to be fairly inexpensive and are suitable for boiling. Collar can also be roasted or braised. Usually they are boned and prepared by the butcher or supermarket and therefore there is little effort involved in cooking them. They can be eaten either hot or cold and there is very little waste on them.

# Hams

Hams are both economical and versatile. Don't fall into the trap of thinking that you can only serve them cold with salad. They can be served hot or cold with a variety of flavorings, glazes and sauces — fruity ones are especially good. Syrup or honey mixed with fruit juices and spices makes a delicious glaze, and should give the meat itself a subtle flavor.

## Ham with Cranberries

**4-lb. fresh cured or cooked ham cloves for decoration**

For the Glaze:
$\frac{1}{4}$ **lb. butter**
$\frac{1}{3}$ **cup corn syrup**
**1 teaspoon cinnamon**
**pinch chili powder**
**1 teaspoon prepared mustard**

For the Cranberry Sauce:
**3 cups cranberries**
**2 tablespoons brown sugar**
$\frac{3}{4}$ **cup water**
**pinch ground ginger**
**1 teaspoon cornstarch**

**1** Soak the ham in cold water overnight. Drain, place in a large saucepan and cover with water. Bring to a boil, then simmer for about $1\frac{1}{4}$ hours. (This step may be eliminated if ham is cooked.)

**2** Remove the ham from the pan and carefully peel off the skin and trim any excess fat. With a knife, make a criss-cross pattern across the fat. Place a clove in the center of each diamond.

**3** Preheat the oven to 350°F.

**4** Make the glaze. Place all the ingredients except the mustard in a pan and bring to a boil. Boil the glaze for 2-3 minutes, then remove from the heat and add the mustard.

**5** Brush the glaze over the ham so that it is coated evenly. Place the ham in a shallow roasting pan and bake in the oven for about 45 minutes until crisp and golden-brown.

**6** Meanwhile, make the cranberry sauce. Place the cranberries, sugar, $\frac{2}{3}$ cup of the water and ginger in a pan and bring to a boil. Boil for 5 minutes. Mix the cornstarch with the remaining water and stir into the sauce. Boil for another 3-4 minutes until the mixture is clear.

**7** Serve the glazed ham hot or cold with the cranberry sauce and cole-slaw.

*Serves 8*

*Glazed Ham with Cranberries has a crisp, golden exterior, studded with cloves, and is served with fresh cranberry sauce*

## Maple Baked Ham

**3-lb. cooked or cured ham**
**1 onion**
**6 peppercorns**
**1 bay leaf**
**cloves for decoration**
**$\frac{1}{3}$ cup maple syrup**
**$\frac{1}{2}$ teaspoon ginger**
**pinch nutmeg**
**pinch allspice**

**1** Place the ham in a large pan, cover with cold water and bring to a boil. Remove the scum from the top and add the onion, peppercorns and bay leaf. Simmer, covered with a lid, for $1\frac{1}{2}$ hours. Cool in the liquid, then drain. (This step may be eliminated if ham is cooked.)

**2** Remove the skin and score the fat in a criss-cross pattern. Stud each diamond shape with a clove.

**3** Preheat the oven to 375°F.

**4** Mix together the maple syrup and spices. Place the ham in a roasting pan and brush with the glaze.

**5** Bake for about 1 hour until the ham is crisp and well glazed.

*Serves 8-10*

## Cinnamon Ham with Apricots

4-lb. cooked ham
½ lb. canned apricot halves, drained

For the Glaze:
1 teaspoon prepared mustard
¼ cup softened butter
3 tablespoons honey
pinch ground cinnamon
pinch ground ginger
2 tablespoons brandy

**1** Preheat the oven to 375°F. Combine the mustard with the softened butter, honey, cinnamon, ginger and brandy. Place the ham in a roasting pan, spread the glazing mixture over the surface of the meat and place in the oven for 5-8 minutes to caramelize the glaze.

**2** Remove the ham from the oven and decorate with the drained apricot halves. Serve cold with a salad of lettuce, celery and apple mixed with a yogurt dressing.

*Serves 8*

**Tip:** A cooked ham can be glazed in a number of ways and is therefore a very versatile dish to prepare. The basic glaze can be varied to include the ingredients you have or the flavors you prefer. In this recipe, for instance, try using a different spirit and change the fruit used for decoration — try peaches, oranges or papayas.

## Ham with Orange

15-lb. fresh or cooked ham
24 cloves
½ cup brown sugar
pinch ground cinnamon
2 teaspoons dry mustard
2¼ cups white wine
bouquet garni

2 onions, sliced
2 carrots, sliced
¼ cup tomato paste
1 tablespoon cider vinegar
3 tablespoons cornstarch
⅔ cup water
4 oranges, sliced
8 candied cherries

**1** Cover the ham with cold water and leave to soak for 6 hours.

**2** Drain and rinse the ham and place it in a large pan. Cover with cold water and bring to a boil, removing any scum as it rises. Simmer for 3½ hours or until tender. (If ham is cooked, steps 1 and 2 may be eliminated.)

**3** Peel off the skin and place the ham in a deep roasting pan. Make sure ham is cool.

**4** Preheat the oven to 350°F. Make regular criss-cross lines, 1 inch apart, on the surface of the ham and press a clove into each intersection.

**5** Mix the sugar, cinnamon and mustard and sprinkle this mixture over the ham. Place in the oven for 1 hour.

**6** After the ham has baked for 20 minutes, pour on the wine and add the bouquet garni, onions, carrots, tomato paste and vinegar and return the pan to the oven for the remaining 40 minutes. Baste the meat frequently to prevent it from drying out.

**7** Lift the ham from the pan and keep it warm while preparing the sauce. Pour the contents of the roasting pan into a saucepan and boil for 10 minutes. Thicken with the cornstarch mixed with the water.

**8** Place the ham on a serving plate and decorate it with the orange slices and cherries. Decorate the end of the bone with a paper cap. Strain the sauce and serve it with the ham.

*Serves 25-30*

**Tip:** Score the oranges from one end to the other before slicing: this will give the slices a decorative serrated edge.

## Ham Mousse

2 tablespoons unflavored gelatin
2 tablespoons medium sherry
⅓ cup stock
1 cup ground cooked ham
⅔ cup white sauce
salt and pepper
pinch grated nutmeg
pinch paprika
⅔ cup heavy cream
1 tablespoon oil

**1** Place the gelatin in a bowl, pour in the sherry and soak for a few minutes to soften the gelatin.

**2** Bring the stock to a boil and pour it over the gelatin. Stir until dissolved.

**3** Stir the ham and the white sauce into the gelatin and stock mixture and then season with salt and pepper. Add a pinch of grated nutmeg and paprika.

**4** Transfer the mixture to a pan and bring to a boil. Simmer for 5 minutes, then cool.

**5** Once the ham mixture is cold, whip the cream until it is stiff and fold it in.

**6** Oil a 3¾-cup mold and place the ham mixture in it. Place in the refrigerator for at least 2 hours to chill it thoroughly.

**7** Turn the mousse onto a flat plate and serve with a salad of lettuce and avocado, garnished with orange and grapefruit sections.

*Serves 4*

*Ham with Orange. What an impressive centerpiece for a buffet or reception — and one you can easily make yourself*

**1** Some of the main ingredients: a fresh ham, salted slab bacon, lettuce, peas, butter, egg, seasoning **2** Place the ham in a pot and cover with water. Bring to a boil, reduce the heat and simmer for 4 hours **3** and **4** Re-

move the brown ends of the lettuce stalks. Peel the carrots and onions. Cut the bacon into strips and cut the carrots into matchsticks. Blanch the bacon strips **5** and **6** Immerse each head of lettuce in boiling water for 2

minutes. Drain. Holding them by the stalks, plunge each one into cold water 3 or 4 times to remove any sand. Drain again, press the leaves together and tie with string

**7** Fry the bacon in a flameproof dish. Arrange the lettuce on top. Cover and cook for 45 minutes **8** Cook the carrots and onions separately in butter and water

10

11

12

**9** Cook the peas in boiling water, flavored with butter, savory, salt and sugar **10** When the ham is cooked, drain it, place it on a board and with a large knife, peel off the skin **11** and **12** Remove the excess fat from the meat. Place the leg in a large roasting pan and pour on the Madeira. Make sure the whole leg has a coating of the wine before baking. Place in the oven to glaze **13** While the ham is cooking, baste it frequently with

13

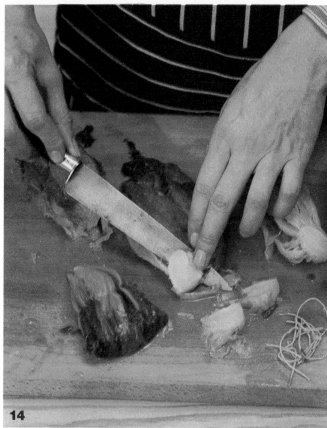

14

15

16

the Madeira. When ready it should have a golden glaze
**14** Halve the lettuces lengthwise. Remove the stalks
carefully with a knife and fold each portion in half
**15** Heat the ham juices with half the cream. Whisk the

remaining cream with the egg yolk and add this to the
sauce **16** Arrange the vegetables around the ham and
serve the peas and sauce separately

# Ham Ile de France

one 13-lb. fresh or cooked ham
6 heads lettuce
1½ lbs. carrots, peeled
½ lb. bacon slab
¼ lb. butter
1 lb. small onions
salt and pepper
1 tablespoon sugar
2 lbs. peas
pinch savory
1¼ cups Madeira
1 cup + 2 tablespoons light
  cream
1 egg yolk

**1** Cover the ham with water and simmer for 4 hours. (This step may be eliminated if a cooked ham is used.)

**2** Trim the stalks of the lettuces. Cut the carrots into matchsticks.

Cut the bacon into strips and blanch in boiling water for 30 seconds. Rinse and drain.

**3** Plunge each head of lettuce into boiling water for 2 minutes and drain. Holding the stalk, dunk each into cold water 3-4 times to remove sand. Press the leaves together firmly and tie with string.

**4** Melt 2 tablespoons butter in a pan. Fry the bacon for 5 minutes, place the lettuces on top, just cover with water and simmer, covered, for 45 minutes.

**5** Place the carrots and onions in separate pans and just cover them with water. Add seasoning, 1 teaspoon sugar and 2 tablespoons butter to each pan. Cover and simmer,

*Cold Glazed Ham is surrounded by orange cups stuffed with rice, olives and fresh fruit in a tangy vinaigrette dressing*

until the water has evaporated. Keep warm. Cook the peas in water seasoned as for the carrots and onions, but add the savory.

**6** Preheat the oven to 375°F. When the ham is cooked, skin it and remove the excess fat. Sprinkle it with Madeira and glaze in the oven for 30 minutes, basting frequently.

**7** Drain and cut the lettuces in half lengthwise. Remove the stalks and fold each portion in half. Place the meat on a serving dish with the lettuce, carrots and onions. Drain the peas and bacon and combine in a bowl.

**8** Pour the ham juices into a pan, add half the cream and boil for 2 minutes. Blend the remaining cream with the egg yolk and gradually stir it into the pan. Season, strain and serve with the meat and vegetables.
*Serves 12-14*

## Cold Glazed Ham

1¼ cups water
2 tablespoons unflavored gelatin
2 tablespoons sugar
1 tablespoon port
salt and pepper
4-lb. cooked ham
1 green leek leaf
4 oranges
4½ cups cooked rice
1 small onion, chopped
8 stuffed green olives chopped
1 teaspoon chopped parsley
2 tablespoons vinaigrette dressing
6 lettuce leaves

**1** Make the aspic: boil the water and remove the pan from the heat. Dissolve the gelatin and sugar in the water. Add the port, season and cool. Brush the ham with half the aspic and allow it to set.

**2** Scald the leek leaf and cut it into strips. Remove the skin from one orange and cut out 25 small petal shapes. Dip these in the remaining aspic and decorate the ham with a floral pattern. Allow to set before recoating the meat.

**3** Making zig-zag incisions, cut 3 oranges into halves. Remove the fruit and white flesh from the skins. Dice the fruit and combine it with the rice, onion, olives, seasoning and parsley. Toss this mixture in the vinaigrette and spoon it into the orange halves.

**4** Place the ham on a bed of lettuce leaves. Surround with the orange salads and serve.

*Serves 6*

## Glazed Ham with Pineapple

3-lb. cooked or fresh ham, halved
bouquet garni
½ cup brown sugar

*Glazed Ham with Pineapple cleverly imitates the real fruit and makes a tasty, attractive dish for buffet parties*

1 tablespoon prepared mustard
¼ lb. butter
1 teaspoon combined allspice and coriander
salt and pepper
cloves for decoration
2 canned pineapple rings
½ lb. canned pineapple chunks, drained

For the Sauce:
¼ cup sugar
¼ cup vinegar
⅓ cup medium sherry
1¼ cups beef stock
⅔ cup pineapple juice
1 tablespoon rum
6 coriander seeds, crushed
2 teaspoons cornstarch
⅓ cup water

**1** Drain and wrap each ham in a piece of cheesecloth. Secure with string. Place them in a large pot and cover with water. Add the bouquet garni, bring to a boil and simmer for 1 hour. Remove from the heat and allow the meat to cool in the liquid. (This step may be eliminated if cooked ham is used.)

**2** Blend the sugar, mustard, butter, mixed spice and seasoning in a bowl.

**3** Drain and dry the hams. Spread them with the glaze and, with a knife, make a lattice pattern all over. Stud each intersection of lines with a clove. Preheat oven to 375°F.

**4** Place them in a roasting tray and braise in the preheated oven for 20 minutes or until the glaze is golden.

**5** While the ham is baking, prepare the sauce. Boil the sugar and vinegar, stirring all the time until the sugar has caramelized. Still stirring, add the sherry, stock, pineapple juice, rum, coriander seeds and seasoning. Boil for 10 minutes and thicken with the cornstarch mixed with the water.

**6** Remove the ham from the oven. Heat the tip of a skewer over a flame and singe the lines of the pattern to a dark brown. (This is optional and purely for decoration.)

**7** Place a pineapple ring on top of each ham, surround with pineapple pieces and serve with the hot sauce.

*Serves 6*

# Fiesta Ham

4-lb. fresh or cooked ham
1¾ cups apple juice
1 onion, finely sliced
freshly ground black pepper
2 tablespoons honey
3 dessert apples
2 tablespoons brown sugar
2 tablespoons butter
2 tablespoons oil
12 stuffed green olives

**1** Cover the ham with cold water and leave to soak for 12 hours. Drain.

**2** Place the ham in a pan and pour on the apple juice. Add the onion and pepper, cover and simmer, allowing 20 minutes per lb. plus 20 minutes.(Steps 1 and 2 may be eliminated if cooked ham is used.)

**3** Preheat the oven to 425°F. Remove the ham from the pan and allow to cool slightly. Remove the skin and score the fat diagonally in a diamond pattern. Place the ham in a shallow ovenproof dish and brush the surface with the honey. Place in the preheated oven for about 15 minutes until golden brown.

**4** Core the apples and, leaving them unpeeled, cut them across in rings. Toss the apple rings in the sugar.

**5** Heat the butter and oil in a pan and fry the apple rings, turning once, until golden.

**6** Place the ham on a serving dish and surround it with the apple rings. Place each olive on a toothpick and push the sticks into the meat in the center of the scored diamond shapes. Serve.

*Serves 10*

**Tips:** Apples combine well with other fruit such as blackberries, currants and black cherries, so try reducing the amount of apple juice and making up the difference with another fruit juice; add a pinch of cinnamon, too. And for more festive occasions, try adding 2 tablespoons apple brandy to the juice.

---

# Mustard Ham

one 12-lb. cooked ham
1¼ cups stock
⅔ cup pineapple juice
¼ cup dry mustard
1 tablespoon cornstarch
2 egg yolks
2 tablespoons Dijon mustard
1½ cups fine dry breadcrumbs

**1** Remove the rind and the most of the fat from the ham and place the meat in a roasting pan. Set the oven temperature to 425°F.

**2** In a bowl, mix the dry mustard, cornstarch, egg yolks and Dijon mustard and beat until smooth. Spread the mixture over the top and sides of the ham.

**3** Sprinkle on the breadcrumbs and place the ham in the oven for about 30 minutes or until the top is browned and crisp.

*Serves 24*

**Tips:** This recipe is sufficient for a large number of people, but if your numbers are smaller, cut the finished ham into 3 and freeze the smaller pieces. If well sealed, the hams should keep for up to 6 months.

---

# Ham Port Maillot

one 5-lb. fresh or cooked ham
salt and pepper
1 lb. carrots, cut in sticks 1½ × ¼ inch
1 lb. turnips, cut in sticks 1½ × ¼ inch
1 lb. green beans
1 lb. frozen peas
1 tablespoon sugar
1¼ cups medium sherry
¼ lb. butter

**1** Cover the ham with cold water and soak for 6 hours, changing the water frequently.

**2** Place the ham in a large pan and cover generously with cold water. Simmer, allowing 40 minutes per 2 lbs. (These first two steps may be eliminated if cooked ham is used.)

**3** Bring a large pan of salted water to a boil, add the carrots and cook for 8 minutes. Add the turnips and cook for a further 5 minutes. Add the beans and peas. When all the vegetables are cooked, drain them, run cold water over them and drain again.

**4** Preheat the oven to 375°F.

**5** Peel off the rind and place the ham in a deep ovenproof dish. Sprinkle it with the sugar and place in the oven for 10 minutes to caramelize the sugar. Pour on the sherry and return to the oven for a further 10-15 minutes, basting occasionally and taking care not to let it burn.

**6** Meanwhile, melt the butter in a pan and add the drained vegetables, salt and pepper. Heat through, stirring from time to time.

**7** Place the ham on a large serving dish, with the vegetables. Pour the sauce from the dish into a sauce boat and serve hot.

*Serves 10–12*

---

*Ham Port Maillot will feed a lot of people, but it can be cooked, cut into smaller pieces and then stored in the freezer*

# Steaks and Slices

Ham and bacon are frequently sold in prepacked slices and "steaks." These cuts are so popular and versatile that they have a permanent place in most household refrigerators. Ham steaks are the leanest and most expensive, but have an excellent flavor. Ham slices vary in size according to the ham they are cut from. As with bacon, the butcher will usually be glad to cut slices to the thickness you need.

## Ham Provençal

1 onion, finely chopped
1 clove of garlic, crushed
¼ cup oil
2 tomatoes, peeled, seeded and chopped
2 teaspoons tomato paste
⅔ cup white wine
salt and black pepper
4 slices ham, about 2-3 ozs. each

1 Sauté the onion and the garlic gently in the oil until soft.

2 Stir in the tomatoes and the tomato paste. Add the white wine and season with salt and freshly ground black pepper. Cook gently for 5 minutes.

3 Roll up the ham slices and place them in the pan, spooning some of the tomato sauce over them. Simmer for 5 minutes more. Serve immediately with boiled noodles or rice.

*Serves 4*

**Tip:** For extra flavor add some chopped fresh herbs, such as parsley, sage and oregano.

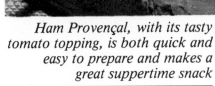

*Ham Provençal, with its tasty tomato topping, is both quick and easy to prepare and makes a great suppertime snack*

## Ham Cordon Bleu

¾ cup chopped mushrooms
1 tablespoon butter
salt and pepper
1 tablespoon chopped fresh parsley and chives
8 slices ham, ¼ inch thick
4 slices cheese, the same size as the ham
2 tablespoons flour
1 large egg, beaten
¾ cup breadcrumbs
¼ cup oil

1 Sauté the mushrooms gently in the butter with a little salt and pepper and the chopped herbs, for 5 minutes. Divide the mushrooms into 4 and spread each part over the middle of a ham slice.

2 Cover the 4 ham and mushroom slices with a slice of cheese to cover the mushrooms. Place the slices under the broiler until the cheese is melted and soft.

3 While the cheese is still hot, place a plain ham slice on top of each one to form a sandwich, stuck together by the melted cheese.

4 Dust each sandwich with seasoned flour and coat with beaten egg and then with breadcrumbs. Fry in the oil until the outside is crisp and golden brown.

*Serves 4*

## Ham and Watercress Cream

2 large or 3 small bunches
  watercress
salt and pepper
$\frac{1}{4}$ cup butter
4 ham steaks
$\frac{2}{3}$ cup light cream

**1** Blanch the watercress in a pan of salted, boiling water for 5 minutes. Drain and rinse well.

**2** Melt the butter in a skillet and fry the ham steaks until just browned. Remove them from the pan and keep them warm.

**3** Add the cress to the pan and sauté over very low heat, stirring frequently, for 15 minutes. Remove from the heat, add salt and pepper and stir in the cream. Serve the ham steaks on a bed of the watercress cream.

*Serves 4*

## Bacon and Onion Tart

one 8-inch pie crust
2 medium onions, sliced
2 tablespoons butter
$\frac{2}{3}$ cup white sauce
1 egg, beaten
1 tablespoon sherry
salt and pepper
$\frac{1}{4}$ lb. sliced bacon

**1** Roll out the dough to line an 8-inch pie plate. Sauté the onions in the butter until soft.

**2** Preheat the oven to 400°F. Combine the white sauce, egg and sherry with seasoning.

**3** Place the bacon on the crust. Cover with the onions and pour on the sauce. Bake for 20 minutes. Then reduce the oven heat to 350°F and cook for another 25 minutes.

*Serves 6*

## Canadian Ham Steaks

$\frac{3}{4}$ cup brown sugar
2 tablespoons flour
2 teaspoons dry mustard
$\frac{1}{4}$ cup vinegar
$\frac{2}{3}$ cup apple juice
3 apples
6 thick ham steaks
2 tablespoons cranberry jelly

**1** Mix together the brown sugar, flour and mustard. Stir in the vinegar and the apple juice to make a smooth sauce.

**2** Peel and core the apples and cut them into slices.

**3** Preheat the oven to 325°F. Place the steaks in a greased ovenproof dish. Cover them with slices of ap-

*Ham and Watercress Cream. The ham and the creamy watercress sauce are cooked in the same pan — simplicity itself!*

ple and pour the sauce over them.

**4** Cover the dish and bake for $\frac{1}{2}$ hour. Remove the lid and bake for another $\frac{1}{2}$ hour, basting from time to time. Serve each ham steak with the sauce and topped with a teaspoonful of the cranberry jelly.

*Serves 6*

**Tips:** Cider may be used in place of the apple juice. For an extra spicy taste, add a pinch each of ground cloves and cinnamon to the mustard.

## Ham Slices au Gratin

12 thin slices of ham
1 cup grated cheese
2 tablespoons butter
freshly ground black pepper

1  On each of the ham slices place a little of the grated cheese. Roll the slices up, enclosing the cheese.

2  Arrange the rolls of ham on a buttered ovenproof dish. Sprinkle the remainder of the grated cheese over the top and dust liberally with freshly ground black pepper.

3  Broil the ham until the cheese is soft and just starting to brown. Serve at once with baked potatoes.

*Serves 6*

**Tip:** The ham rolls may be filled with cooked spinach, celery hearts or asparagus tips. To add moisture sprinkle with sherry or vermouth while cooking.

*Ham Slices au Gratin are easy to prepare and make a tasty supper snack when you want to treat your family and friends*

## Ham Steaks with Pears

2 tablespoons butter
1 teaspoon honey
grated rind 1 orange
pinch cinnamon
4 ham steaks
2 pears

1  Cream together the butter, honey, orange rind and cinnamon.

2  Preheat the oven to 400°F.

3  Arrange the ham steaks in a greased ovenproof dish. Spread the butter mixture over the top of them. Bake for 12 minutes.

4  Remove from the oven. Peel the pears, cut them in half and remove the cores. Place a half pear on top of each glazed ham steak and serve.

*Serves 4*

**Tips:** A teaspoonful of mild mustard may be added to the glaze for extra tang.

Peaches, apricots, or fresh pineapple slices may be substituted for the pear halves.

If the ham is very salty or dry, poach the steaks in meat stock for 10 minutes before cooking. Soaking the steaks in cold water for an hour before cooking will also remove excess salt.

## Ham Steak Charcutière

2 tablespoons oil
1 large onion, chopped
1 tablespoon flour
1 tablespoon tomato paste
1¼ cups stock
salt and pepper
sprig thyme
1 tablespoon capers
1 small dill pickle, cut in matchstick strips

560

1 small cooked beet, cut in match-
stick-sized strips
1 teaspoon vinegar
1 teaspoon honey
4 thick ham steaks

**1** Heat the oil and sauté the onion until soft. Stir in the flour and cook for 2-3 minutes. Add the tomato paste and the stock. Season lightly and add the thyme. Bring to a boil, and simmer briskly for 15-20 minutes to make a sauce.

**2** Strain the sauce, season to taste and stir in the capers, pickle, beet, vinegar and honey. Cook for 5 minutes.

**3** Heat the ham steaks under the broiler and arrange them on a serving dish. Pour the sauce over them and serve.

*Serves 4*

---

*Ham and Fennel Rolls — slices of ham filled with a superb fennel, bacon and wine sauce and then topped with melted cheese*

# Ham and Fennel Rolls

2 medium fennel bulbs
¼ cup oil
¼ lb. lean bacon, sliced
1 large onion, finely chopped
1 tablespoon flour
3 tomatoes, peeled, seeded and
   chopped
½ cup white wine
1¼ cups stock
1 clove garlic, crushed
bouquet garni
salt and pepper
¾ cup grated Gruyère cheese
4 large slices ham

**1** Clean the fennel and cut each bulb in quarters. Boil them in salted water for 8 minutes, drain and rinse in cold water.

**2** Heat half the oil in a skillet and sauté the fennel until golden, turning the pieces frequently. Cover the pan and cook over low heat until tender. Remove from the pan and keep warm.

**3** Add the rest of the oil to the pan and fry the bacon and onion until just browned. Stir in the flour and cook until just colored.

**4** Stir in the tomatoes and cook for 1 minute. Add the wine and stock, garlic and bouquet garni, and season. Simmer for 20 minutes.

**5** Preheat the oven to 400°F. Pass the sauce through a strainer or food mill. Mix half the sauce with the fennel and stir in the grated cheese; cook gently for 5 minutes.

**6** Butter an ovenproof dish. On the slices of ham place ¼ of the fennel mixture. Roll the ham slices around the fennel and arrange the rolls in the dish. Pour on the rest of the sauce and sprinkle with the remainder of the grated cheese. Bake for 10 minutes until golden. Serve hot.

*Serves 4*

# Ham with Chablis

1½ teaspoons butter
four ¼-inch thick slices cooked
  ham
¾ cup Chablis or other dry white
  wine
3¾ cups trimmed and finely sliced
  mushrooms
1 clove garlic, chopped
2 shallots, chopped
salt and pepper
1 cup sour cream

**1** Preheat the oven to 400°F.

**2** Butter an ovenproof dish and place the slices of ham in it. Pour in ¼ cup of the Chablis, cover the dish and place in the oven for 10 minutes.

**3** Place the mushrooms, garlic and shallots in a sauté pan, pour on the rest of the wine and season. Bring quickly to a boil, then simmer for 10 minutes.

**4** Add the sour cream and boil for 5 minutes.

**5** Remove the ham from the oven and add the cooking juices to the mushrooms. Boil the sauce again for 5 minutes.

**6** Place the slices of ham in a deep serving dish, pour on the sauce and serve hot.

*Serves 4*

---

# Cranberry Glazed Ham

2 tablespoons melted butter
2 teaspoons prepared mustard
black pepper
4 ham steaks
1 cup cranberries
1 cup sugar
grated rind and juice 1 orange

**1** Mix the butter, mustard and pepper. Brush the steaks with the mixture and broil on one side for 5 minutes. Turn over, brush again and broil until tender.

**2** Mix the cranberries, sugar and orange rind and juice in a pan. Let

*Ham Florentine. The slices of ham surround a spinach and cream filling and are served with a rich, Madeira-flavored sauce*

stand for 5 minutes.

**3** Simmer the cranberries gently for 5 minutes or until they pop.

**4** Garnish the ham with the cranberries and serve with noodles.

*Serves 4*

---

# Ham Florentine

2 tablespoons oil
¼ cup butter
1 carrot, diced
1 onion, chopped
2 slices of lean bacon, cut in pieces
2 tablespoons flour
1¼ cups chicken stock
½ cup Madeira
salt and pepper
pinch thyme
1 bay leaf
4 lbs. spinach, cooked and
  chopped
½ cup heavy cream
6 thick slices cooked ham

**1** Heat the oil with half the butter and sauté the carrot, onion and bacon until slightly browned. Sprinkle in the flour and cook for 2 minutes more, stirring. Mix in the stock and Madeira, season and add the thyme and bay leaf. Cover and cook for 25 minutes.

**2** Preheat the oven to 400°F. Mix the spinach with the cream and seasoning. Divide the spinach between the slices of ham and roll them up. Place in an ovenproof dish greased with the rest of the butter.

**3** Strain the sauce and pour half over the rolls. Place in the oven for 10 minutes, then serve with the rest of the sauce.

*Serves 6*

---

*Ham with Chablis is expensive to make but never fails to impress your guests at that special occasion or dinner*

# Ham and Leek Mornay

4 young leeks
4 large slices ham
2 tablespoons butter
1¼ cups white sauce
1 cup grated Cheddar cheese
salt and pepper

**1** Preheat the oven to 375°F. Trim and remove the outer leaves of the leeks. Cut off the green part and cook the white part for 15 minutes in boiling salted water.

**2** Roll a slice of ham around each leek. Grease a shallow ovenproof casserole dish with half the butter, and place the leeks inside. Add ¾ cup of the cheese to the white sauce and season it.

**3** Pour the cheese sauce over the leeks. Sprinkle with the remaining cheese and dot with the rest of the butter.

**4** Bake in the preheated oven for 15 minutes and serve.

*Serves 4*

---

# Ham and Apple Casserole

¼ cup butter
2 onions, sliced
2 apples, peeled, cored and sliced
4 ham steaks
¼ cup flour
1¼ cups cider
⅔ cup chicken stock
salt and pepper
pinch ground cloves
½ teaspoon dry mustard
2 cups canned corn, drained
½ cup raisins
1½ cups mushrooms, washed and sliced

**1** Preheat the oven to 375°F. Melt the butter in a pan. Sauté the onions and apples until soft. Add the ham slices and brown on both sides. Transfer the ham to a flame-proof casserole.

**2** Add the flour to the pan and stir over low heat for 2 minutes. Add the cider and stock and bring to a boil, stirring all the time.

**3** Simmer and add the seasoning, mustard, corn, raisins and mushrooms. Cook for 1 more minute and pour the contents of the pan into the casserole dish. Cover and cook in the oven for 45 minutes or until well cooked.

*Serves 4*

---

# Ham Jambalaya

¼ cup oil
1 lb. cooked ham, diced
1 onion, finely chopped
2 cloves garlic, crushed
1 tomato, peeled, seeded, and chopped
2 cups long grain rice
3 cups water
1 chicken bouillon cube
pinch turmeric
salt and pepper
14 ozs. canned pineapple chunks with their juice
1 cup peeled shrimp
1 egg
⅔ cup fine dry breadcrumbs
2 tablespoons butter

**1** Heat the oil in a saucepan, add the ham and fry gently for 5 minutes. Add the onion, garlic and tomato and sauté for 5 more minutes. Add the rice, water, stock cube, turmeric, salt and pepper.

**2** Drain the pineapple pieces, and retain ⅔ cup of the juice. Add this to the pan.

**3** Bring to a boil, cover and cook gently for 15 minutes.

**4** Stir in the shrimp and heat through. Check the seasoning. Place the rice on a serving dish.

**5** Dry the pineapple pieces. Beat the egg. Dip the pineapple in the egg and roll each piece in the breadcrumbs.

**6** Melt the butter in a skillet, add the pineapple pieces and fry until golden on both sides.

**7** Spoon the pineapple onto the rice and serve.

*Serves 6*

---

# Ham with Wine and Tomato

¼ cup butter
6 large slices cooked ham
6 shallots, chopped
⅓ cup dry white wine
4 tomatoes, skinned, seeded and chopped
2 teaspoons tomato paste
salt and pepper
⅔ cup heavy cream
1 sprig parsley

**1** Preheat the oven to 375°F. Butter a small baking dish. Roll the ham slices into cylinders and place them side by side in the dish. Dot the ham with 1 tablespoon of butter and place it in the oven for 15 minutes or until heated through.

**2** Meanwhile, gently melt the remaining butter in a skillet and sauté the shallots for 3 minutes.

**3** Add the wine and boil for 2 minutes before adding the tomatoes and tomato paste. Season. Allow the sauce to boil for 5 more minutes while gradually stirring in the cream. Check the seasoning.

**4** Pour the sauce over the ham, and garnish with the parsley.

*Serves 6*

---

*Ham with Wine and Tomato is served with a quickly prepared onion and tomato sauce which is enriched with wine and cream*

# Ham Shank

A shank is the hind leg taken from a side of bacon. It is sometimes sold whole, but it can also be cut into smaller pieces and slices.

## Champagne Shank

4-lb. ham shank, soaked overnight
2¼ cups water
2¼ cups sparkling cider
bouquet garni
1 onion
cloves for decoration
⅓ cup honey

2 tablespoons brown sugar
juice and grated rind 1 orange
1 teaspoon combined allspice and coriander
1 teaspoon prepared mustard

**1** Drain the shank, place it in a pan and add the water, cider, bouquet garni and onion. Bring to a boil and simmer for 1¼ hours.

**2** Remove the pan from the heat and allow the meat to cool in the stock for 1 hour. Lift out the shank, and reserve some of the stock.

**3** Score criss-cross lines in the rind and press the cloves into the grooves.

**4** Preheat the oven to 350°F. Place the remaining ingredients in a pan and warm gently to melt. Place the ham in a roasting pan and coat evenly with the honey mixture. Place in the oven for 20 minutes, basting with a little of the stock.

---

*Shank with Pineapple and Apricots. The sweet jam glaze and the sharp fruit garnish make a mouthwatering combination*

**5** Decorate the shank with a paper frill and serve garnished with halved oranges topped with candied cherries.

*Serves 8–10*

## Ham Shank with Pineapple and Apricots

one 4-5 lb. ham shank
6 tablespoons apricot jam
2 tablespoons prepared mustard
cloves for decoration
1 small fresh pineapple, peeled
1 tablespoon chutney
¼ cup unsweetened pineapple juice
2 lbs. canned apricot halves, drained

**1** Cover the ham with cold water and soak for 4 hours.

**2** Preheat the oven to 375°F. Drain the ham and wrap it in aluminum foil. Place in a roasting pan and bake in the preheated oven for 2 hours.

**3** Remove the rind from the ham and score the surface of the meat. Mix half the apricot jam with the mustard and spread the mixture over the ham. Stud the meat with the cloves in a decorative pattern and return it to the oven for about 30 minutes.

**4** Meanwhile, cut the pineapple into slices and remove the core from each slice. Heat the remaining apricot jam with the chutney and pineapple juice in a wide pan. Glaze the pineapple slices and the apricot halves in this mixture.

**5** Place the finished ham on a serving dish and garnish with the pineapple slices and apricot halves.

*Serves 10*

---

*Champagne Shank is simple yet effective. It is cooked in sparkling cider and coated in a mustard and honey glaze*

## Swedish Ham Salad

4 small ham slices
2 tablespoons melted butter
2 medium cooking apples
1 tablespoon sugar
pinch grated nutmeg
1 cup mayonnaise
1 teaspoon prepared mustard
salt and pepper
½ white cabbage, finely shredded
1 carrot, grated
2 tablespoons raisins
2 dessert apples
juice 1 lemon

1 Remove the rind from the ham and broil for 10 minutes on each side, brushing with melted butter. Cool completely.

2 Peel, core and slice the cooking apples and put in a small pan with the sugar and 1 tablespoon water. Cover the pan and cook for 12-15 minutes until they are soft. Add the nutmeg and mash well with a fork. Leave to cool.

3 When the apple purée is cold, stir in the mayonnaise, mustard and seasoning to taste.

4 Mix the white cabbage, carrot and raisins. Quarter the dessert apples, remove the core and dice. Toss the apple in the lemon juice, then add the apple and juice to the cabbage mixture.

5 Arrange the cabbage salad in a serving dish. Top with the cold ham slices and coat with the apple mayonnaise.

6 Serve cold.

*Serves 4*

**Tip:** A variety of additions can be made to the raw cabbage salad according to your taste. Try adding a little grated onion, chopped mandarin orange, cooked peas or sweet corn, thinly sliced green pepper, chopped tomato or even a little grated cheese.

## Brazilian Ham Shank and Beans

2-lb. ham shank, soaked overnight
1 lb. kidney beans, soaked overnight
2 tablespoons oil
3 onions, chopped
3 cloves garlic, crushed
1 teaspoon dry mustard
1 tablespoon chopped parsley
2 teaspoons chopped chives
juice 1 lemon
6 tomatoes, skinned, seeded and chopped
dash chili sauce
1 bay leaf
2 pork and beef sausages
2 small pork sausages
pepper

1 Drain and rinse the soaked ham and place in it a pan. Cover with cold water, bring to a boil, skim the surface and simmer gently for 1 hour.

2 Drain and rinse the soaked beans and place them in a separate pan. Cover with cold water, bring to a boil, skim the surface and simmer gently for 1 hour.

3 Heat the oil in a skillet and sauté the onions and garlic until soft but not brown. Add the mustard, parsley, chives, lemon juice, chopped tomatoes, chili sauce and bay leaf, and cook for 5 minutes.

4 Drain the beans and ham and put them together in a large pan with the tomato mixture, sausages and pepper to taste. Just cover with water, bring to a boil and simmer over low heat for about 1½ hours, until the meat and beans are tender. Add water if necessary.

5 Serve hot with side dishes of sliced orange, fried banana, cooked green cabbage and boiled rice.

*Serves 8*

**Tip:** This dish is adapted from a traditional Brazilian recipe called Feijoada, which includes the hocks, ears, tongue, dried meat and several types of bacon. Brazilian Ham and Beans has the same spicy flavor as the original dish, but uses readily available ingredients.

## Ham Shank Casserole

1½ lbs. lean ham shank cut into ¾-inch cubes
2 tablespoons lard or shortening
1 large onion, peeled and sliced
2 branches celery, sliced
¾ cup long grain rice
1 chicken bouillon cube, dissolved in 1¾ cups boiling water
1 cup canned tomatoes in juice
1 bay leaf
¼ teaspoon oregano
¼ teaspoon marjoram
pinch cinnamon
salt and pepper
1½ cups mushrooms
½ lb. canned butter beans

1 Preheat the oven to 325°F. Fry the ham in the melted fat until sealed on all sides. Remove with slotted spoon to a casserole.

2 Add the onion and celery to the pan and sauté until soft. Stir in the rice and sauté gently for 3 minutes. Add the stock, tomatoes and juice, herbs, cinnamon and seasoning. Bring to a boil, pour over the ham and stir well.

3 Cover and cook in the preheated oven for 1 hour, fluffing up the rice with a fork occasionally.

4 Add the trimmed mushrooms and butter beans and continue to cook for 30 minutes.

*Serves 6*

*Brazilian Ham Shank and Beans. Our version uses kidney beans, but any other dried beans would be equally delicious*

## Ham and Olives en Croûte

2-lb. fresh ham, soaked overnight
1 lb. frozen puff pastry, thawed
2 tablespoons brown sugar
2 teaspoons French-style mustard
8 stuffed green olives, chopped
a little beaten egg

**1** Place the soaked ham in a saucepan. Cover with cold water, bring to a boil and simmer for 1 hour.

**2** Remove the ham from the pan and cool slightly. Remove the skin and excess fat and allow to cool completely.

**3** Preheat the oven to 425°F. Roll the pastry out to a circle large enough to wrap the ham.

**4** Mix the sugar, mustard and olives and spread on top of the ham. Place it sugar side down on the pastry. Fold the pastry up over the ham, sealing the seams together with beaten egg.

**5** Place the ham, seams downward, on a flat baking sheet. Make a small hole in the top and decorate with leaves made from pastry trimmings. Brush with egg.

**6** Bake for 25-30 minutes, until the pastry is golden.

*Serves 6*

---

*Ham and Olives en Croûte proves how versatile ham can be, and looks and tastes good as well as being economical*

## Ham and Chestnuts en Croûte

3-lb. fresh ham, soaked overnight, or cooked ham
1 tablespoon butter
1 onion, chopped
1 cup canned unsweetened chestnut purée
¼ cup crunchy peanut butter
¼ teaspoon chopped fresh thyme
pinch ground cloves and allspice together
salt and pepper
2 teaspoons honey
2 eggs, beaten
1½ lb. frozen puff pastry, thawed

**1** Place the soaked ham in a saucepan. Cover with cold water, bring to a boil and simmer for 1½ hours. (This step may be eliminated if a cooked ham is used).

**2** Remove the ham from the pan. Cool. Remove the skin and excess fat and cool completely.

**3** Preheat the oven to 425°F. Melt the butter in a small pan and saute the onion until soft. Drain and mix with the chestnut purée, peanut butter, thyme, spice, seasoning, honey and half of the beaten egg to bind.

**4** Roll the pastry out to a circle large enough to wrap the ham.

**5** Spread the mixture over the top and sides of the ham and place it, chestnut side down, on the pastry. Fold the pastry up over the ham, sealing the seams together with a little beaten egg.

**6** Turn onto a flat baking sheet. Make a small hole in the top and decorate with leaves made from pastry trimmings. Brush all over with beaten egg.

**7** Bake for 30-35 minutes, or until the pastry is golden brown.

*Serves 8–10*

---

*Ham and Chestnuts en Croûte is a welcome change from the usual Sunday ham — serve it hot with a delicious brown gravy*

## Broiled Bacon

For perfect broiled slices, cook them on a rack, under medium heat at first to be sure that they don't curl up, then crisp them under a hot broiler. Ham steaks are also suitable for this method of cooking — place them under high heat for 4 or 5 minutes on each side, and serve with a spoonful of pickle or a pineapple slice. Bacon has a high proportion of fat, so when broiling there's no need to add any.

Broiled bacon slices are delicious served in a mixed grill with liver, sausages and tomatoes; with mushrooms in a hot sandwich, with pancakes, waffles or French toast.

### Herby Kebabs

½ lb. pork tenderloin
2 onions, peeled and sliced
2 fresh sage leaves, chopped, or
  ½ teaspoon dried
¼ cup brandy
¼ cup oil
salt and pepper
4 tomatoes
2 cloves garlic, crushed
2 tablespoons dry white wine
½ teaspoon dried thyme
¼ teaspoon dried basil
1 teaspoon paprika
½ lb. lean bacon slices
½ green pepper, cut into 1-inch
  cubes
8 pearl onions, peeled
8 small fresh bay leaves
¾ cup long grain rice

**1** Cut the pork into 1-inch cubes and place in a dish with the onion, sage, brandy and 2 tablespoons of the oil. Season and marinate for 12 hours.

*Herby Kebabs includes the recipe for a deliciously different tomato sauce — try them both at your next barbecue*

**2** Make the sauce, reserving 2 small tomatoes for the kebabs. Skin and seed the tomatoes and chop the flesh.

**3** Heat 1 tablespoon of the oil in a pan, add the tomatoes, garlic, wine, thyme, basil, paprika and salt to taste and simmer gently for 25 minutes. Pass it through a food mill or blend, and return to the pan.

**4** Remove the rind, if any, from the bacon slices, and roll them up tightly. Cut the 2 reserved tomatoes into quarters. Put the pepper and onions into boiling, salted water and boil for 3 minutes. Drain and rinse in cold water.

**5** Thread the pork, bacon, tomato, pepper, onions and bay leaves onto 4 long skewers.

**6** Put the rice into a pan with 1¾ cups cold salted water. Bring to a boil, cover and cook very gently for about 20 minutes until liquid is absorbed.

**7** Cook the kebabs under a very hot broiler for about 10 minutes, until the meat is cooked through. Turn the kebabs frequently and brush with the marinade and the remaining oil.

**8** Arrange a little cooked rice on a heated serving dish. Arrange the

2 tablespoons oil
salt and cayenne pepper
6 slices lean bacon

**1** Remove the pits from the soaked prunes.

**2** Fry the almonds for 2 or 3 minutes in the hot oil, until golden brown. Drain and toss in a little salt and cayenne pepper. Put the almonds inside the prunes.

**3** Remove the rind from the bacon, if any, stretch the slices with the back of a knife. Cut them in half and wrap each half around a stuffed prune. Secure with toothpicks or small wooden skewers.

**4** Broil under medium heat until the bacon is golden brown all over, turning occasionally. Serve immediately.

*Makes 12*

**Tip:** These make delicious cocktail tidbits or after-dinner savories. You may substitute water chestnuts, scallops, cooked cocktail sausages or frankfurter pieces for the cooked prunes in this recipe.

kebabs on top and moisten them with some of the reheated tomato sauce. Serve the remaining rice and sauce separately.

*Serves 4*

## Snacktime Treats

**8 frozen fish sticks**
**2 tablespoons tartar sauce**
**8 slices lean bacon,**

**1** Spread the fish sticks with tartar sauce. Wrap one slice of bacon around each.

*Devils on Horseback are filled bacon rolls. Our recipe uses prunes and nuts but gives some other tasty variations*

**2** Broil under medium heat for 10-15 minutes until cooked, turning frequently.

*Serves 4*

## Devils on Horseback

**12 large prunes, soaked overnight**
**12 blanched almonds**

**Crumbled Bacon Bits**
Broil slices of bacon until they are crisp and golden. Drain them on absorbent paper and crumble roughly. Add this to savory dips for a smoky bacon flavor . . . mix it with grated cheese, pile onto halved tomatoes and place under the broiler until the cheese is bubbling and golden . . . add to cheese sauce to pour over cooked cauliflower for a special lunch dish . . . mix with grated cheese, a little tomato catsup and a pinch of herbs, spread on toast and broil until melted for a quick and tasty pizza . . . scoop out cooked baked potatoes, add the bacon and some crumbled cheese and place it back in the oven to melt . . . mix it into your favorite pancake, crêpe or waffle batter for a breakfast-time treat.

# Economy Bacon and Ham

Ham and bacon are among the most economical of meats. They are cheaper than many other cuts and their dense, well-flavored texture goes further. They can be re-cooked, and leftovers can be used in many delicious ways. Cooked bacon and ham will keep well in the refrigerator but should be cooked and eaten quickly once removed.

## Ham and Cheese Eggplant

4 eggplants
salt and pepper
2 onions, chopped
¼ cup oil
1 lb. leftover ham or broiled bacon, diced
1 cup grated cheese
1 tablespoon chopped parsley

**1** Slice the eggplants in half lengthwise. Salt the cut side and leave for 1 hour. Rinse off the salt and bitter juices. Scoop out the pulp in the middle of the slices, leaving about ½ inch thickness of pulp inside the skin. Reserve the pulp.

**2** Preheat oven to 350°F. Sauté the onions gently in the oil until soft. Stir in the eggplant; cook for 5 minutes. Add the diced, cooked meat and cook for 3 minutes. Season with salt and pepper.

**3** Fill the hollowed eggplant skins with the mixture and place them on a large, shallow ovenproof dish. Sprinkle the tops with grated cheese and parsley. Bake in the oven for 30 minutes. Serve hot.

*Serves 8*

## Stuffed Cabbage with Ham

1 large cabbage
2 tablespoons butter
2 medium onions, finely chopped
1 shallot, chopped (optional)
1 lb. leftover boiled ham or boiled beef
½ lb. lean bacon
few sprigs parsley
1 cup fresh breadcrumbs
¼ cup milk
1 egg
salt and pepper
pinch garlic salt
1¼ cups stock

**1** Break or cut the leaves of the cabbage away cleanly at the base, so as not to tear them. Wash. Plunge them into boiling salted water for 3 minutes to make them just pliable but not soft. Drain and rinse them in cold water.

**2** Melt the butter and sauté the chopped onions and shallot (if used) until soft but not browned.

**3** Grind the meats with the parsley. Soak the breadcrumbs in the milk, squeezing out any excess. Add the egg, soaked breadcrumbs and fried onions to the meat mixture, and season. Blend to combine the ingredients evenly to a smooth thick paste. Check the seasoning.

**4** Preheat the oven to 350°F.

**5** On a clean cloth arrange the cabbage leaves in an overlapping circle, the largest leaves first. Spoon the stuffing into the middle of the leaves. Carefully fold the leaves over the stuffing as if wrapping a parcel, until the stuffing is completely covered.

**6** With kitchen string, tie the cabbage around the middle, then at right angles to the first string, and then through the quadrants, so that the leaves cannot fall away from the stuffing. Place the stuffed cabbage in an ovenproof dish and pour on the stock. Cover and bake for 1½ hours, removing the lid after the first hour and basting regularly to brown the top of the cabbage.

Serve cut in wedges, with the cooking juices as a gravy.

*Serves 6–8*

## Burgundian Ham

2-lb. fresh ham
2 calves feet
1 onion, peeled
1 carrot, quartered
10 peppercorns in cheesecloth
1¼ cups dry white wine
2½ cups clear light stock
bouquet garni
2 tablespoons white wine vinegar
salt and pepper

**1** Rid the ham of excess salt by soaking it for 2-3 hours in water.

**2** Place the ham and the calves feet in cold unsalted water with the onion, carrot and peppercorns. Bring to a boil, and skim off any scum that forms on the surface. Simmer for ½ hour. Remove ham and calves feet from the water.

**3** On a carving board cut the rind and any bone away from the ham, and dice the meat. Remove the bone from the calves feet. Place the ham and boned calves feet in a clean pan and cover with the white wine and stock. Add the bouquet garni and peppercorns.

**4** Bring to a boil quickly, cover with a lid, and simmer over very low even heat for 2 hours to form a very clear stock.

**5** Remove the ham pieces from the stock and flake the meat. Place it in a salad dish and strain the stock through a fine strainer over it. Stir in the vinegar and chopped parsley. Leave it to gel for several hours or overnight in the refrigerator. To serve, put on a platter and cut in thick slices.

*Serves 8*

# Look 'n Cook Stuffed Cabbage with Bacon

**1** The ingredients **2** Blanch the cabbage leaves. Rinse **3** Soften the onion in butter **4** Grind the meat and parsley together. Soak the breadcrumbs in the milk **5** Add the egg, onion and breadcrumbs. Blend lightly to combine all the ingredients. Season **6** Arrange the cabbage leaves in an overlapping circle on a clean cloth. Spoon stuffing into the middle **7** Fold over the leaves to enclose the stuffing. Tie at 8 points with kitchen string **8** Place in an ovenproof dish with stock, cover and bake **9** Remove string. Serve cut in wedges with the cooking juices as a gravy

# Smoked Ham

Salted and smoked hams, including Virginia, Kentucky and Dijon, are boiled to serve either hot or cold as a much-prized dish. The curing of hams is a very specialized industry. The meat is covered with a mixture of salt, saltpeter and sugar and left for three days. It is then put into brine, washed and dried and finally smoked in a special chamber. It is usually necessary to soak smoked ham before cooking in order to remove the very salty flavor.

The best known and most popular variety of smoked ham is prosciutto from Parma in Italy. These pigs are fed on whey from the local cheese which contributes to its delicate flavor. Parma ham (prosciutto) can be bought in the delicatessen section, thinly sliced and ready to eat without further preparation or cooking. It must be kept well-covered in the refrigerator to prevent it from drying out.

**Parma Ham Antipasto**
Wafer-thin slices of translucent smoked ham wrapped loosely around fresh fruits must be the most refreshing and simple appetizer.

The ingredients should be touched as little as possible and served right away for them to be seen and eaten at their best. Each of the following fruit preparations is enough for 4 servings.

**1** Peel 1 large or 2 small papayas, seed and cut into wedges. Wrap 1 or 2 slices of ham around each and garnish with thin slices of lemon and parsley sprigs.

**2** Cut 8 fresh figs in half. Form 4 ham slices into cornet shapes and fill and garnish with the halved figs.

**3** Remove the peel and seeds from half a small ripe honeydew melon. Slice it into 4 wedges and garnish each wedge with 1 or 2 slices ham and thinly sliced orange.

**4** Halve two tiny cantaloupes, deseed and garnish each with 1 slice ham and a few seedless green grapes.

**5** Peel 1 avocado, cut it into quarters lengthwise and brush it with lemon juice to keep it white. Arrange each quarter on a plate with 1

*Parma Ham Antipasto is a tasty, traditional northern Italian appetizer which can be served with figs, melon slices or papayas*

or 2 slices ham and garnish with black olives.

**6** Peel 2 dessert pears, cut them in half lengthwise and remove the core using a teaspoon. Brush each half with lemon juice, fill with halved and deseeded black grapes and arrange each on a plate with a cornet of ham.

**7** Peel and halve 2 peaches or nectarines, roll 1 or 2 slices ham around each half and garnish with tiny sprigs of watercress.

**8** Halve 4 dessert plums and remove the pits. Arrange on the plate with slices of ham and garnish with orange sections.